African American Awareness
for Young Children

A CURRICULUM

By Dr. Evia L. Davis

Good Year Books

An Imprint of Addison-Wesley Educational Publishers, Inc.

Dedicated to my children:

Nicole Titilayo Davis
Mark Hosea Davis II

Acknowledgments

In all thy ways acknowledge Him and He shall direct thy paths.—Proverbs 3:6

A special thank you to my husband, Dr. Mark H. Davis, for his guidance, support, and constant prayers.

Good Year Books are available for most basic curriculum subjects plus many enrichment areas. For more Good Year Books, contact your local bookseller or educational dealer. For a complete catalog with information about other Good Year Books, please write to:

Good Year Books
1900 East Lake Avenue
Glenview, Illinois 60025

Design and Interior Illustration: Nancy Rudd
Cover Illustration: Sue Shanahan

PHOTO CREDITS
Unless otherwise credited, all photographs are the property of Addison-Wesley Educational Publishers, Inc.

14 Madame C.J. Walker Collection, Indiana Historical Society. 18 U.S. Patent and Trademark Office. 22 U.S. Patent and Trademark Office. 26 Courtesy of Murray Kaufmann and Marjory G. Blubaugh. 30 The Western Reserve Historical Society. 34 Courtesy of Provident Hospital, Chicago. 38 NASA. 44 AP/Wide World. 52 California State University, Long Beach. 56 AP/Wide World. 60 Stock Montage, Inc. 64 U.S. Postal Service. 70 AP/Wide World. 76 U.S. Patent Office and Trademark Office. 80 U.S. Patent and Trademark Office. 84 U.S. Postal Service. 90 U.S. Patent and Trademark Office. 108 Courtesy Dr. Evia L. Davis.

Contents

Contents *(continued)*

African American Awareness for Young Children, Copyright © 1999 Good Year Books.

Introduction

A merican schools have a challenge and responsibility to educate all children so that they truly understand themselves in comparison to other cultures. This responsibility extends to helping children realize their own self-concepts, and to helping them deal with social issues and problems that arise and threaten those self-concepts. Children become aware of racial differences at an early age. Therefore, schools and parents are wise to begin instruction early and provide positive modeling regarding race relations. Young children should begin to explore instructional materials reflecting a multiethnic world as part of their earliest school experience. Children of all races benefit from such experiences. All children should be provided with models in literature with whom they can identify, as well as be exposed to literature that helps them begin to develop understanding and respect for other people and their cultures.

This book, *African American Awareness for Young Children*, provides a curriculum for a study of African American awareness suitable for grades pre-kindergarten to 1. Specifically, the curriculum will assist teachers in developing lesson plans, as well as provide a partial listing of relevant materials and children's books depicting the African American experience. Although this is an African American awareness program, the intent is for it to be used within an integrated setting. Over the years research has shown that there are benefits received from teaching this type of program in a mixed-race class, rather than solely to African American children. Some of the benefits are (1) children become more knowledgeable about people who may or may not be different from themselves, (2) knowledge breeds understanding that allows children's self-esteem and sense of culture to be strengthened, and (3) the end result of it all is that children learn and are encouraged to live in peace and harmony with their neighbors (locally and globally). This listing is by no means exhaustive.

The curriculum includes activities designed to promote the physical, social, emotional, and cognitive development of young children.

Lesson plans are centered around the following themes:

Chapter 1. *The Family*

Chapter 2. *Exploring the Community*

Chapter 3. *Social Interaction*

Chapter 4. *African American Inventors*

Research proves that when teaching children about their heritage and building self-esteem, a good starting point is the family and then the world around them. Therefore, this book starts with the family, then explores the community, and then the social interactions among children. It is also helpful for children to learn about the contributions made by men and women of their culture. The data makes plain the view that children should know the contributions and inventions of past and present African American heroes (as well as those of other ethnic groups). Therefore, this book studies the African American contributions and inventions and gives children positive role models, such as astronaut Mae Jemison. The inventions chosen for the book were based on items familiar to most young children, are a part of everyday living, and are developmentally appropriate for the young mind.

Finally, the appendix includes lists of valuable reference materials, including African American children's books, African American illustrators, African American publishers, and catalog publishers and suppliers for products of particular interest to African Americans.

Each chapter is set up the same way for ease of use. First, the objectives of the chapter are stated. Next, suggestions are given for children's storybooks to introduce the concepts, with each story reference including a short synopsis of its content. The lessons that follow include a biography and a portrait of the person being studied, as available, and a lesson chock-full of activities. Most lessons include either a coloring page or a pattern for making projects.

The coloring page can be assigned at school or offered for take-home. It also serves as a notice to parents, so they can see what the child is studying and can help reinforce the teaching. Each coloring page includes a short description of the person being studied and their contribution.

African American Awareness for Young Children. Copyright © 1999 Good Year Books.

Chapter 1

The Family

This unit consists of five lessons on identifying family members, with activities to assist children in understanding the concept of mother, father, boy, girl, and baby. Moreover, the lesson leads children to understand that they are members of a family. A short synopsis is provided about each suggested story. Lessons are developmentally appropriate and are based on research findings that indicate children can benefit from explicit cognitive training at very early age levels. Skills are embedded into each lesson's activities.

OBJECTIVES

1. To promote a sense of identity and responsibility as a family member

2. To recognize storytelling as an important part of transmitting African American culture

3. To help children develop a positive self-concept

4. To encourage children to identify family members (mother, sister, brother, father, grandmother, etc.)

Story Time

Clifton, Lucille
Everett Anderson's Nine Month Long

Everett and his family expect the birth of their newest member.

Greenfield, Eloise
She Come Bringing Me That Little Baby Girl

Kevin's frustration and jealousy of his new baby sister are dissolved as his role becomes clear.

Johnson, Angela
Do Like Kyla

An expression of love between two sisters

Keats, Ezra Jack
Whistle for Willie

Willie learns to whistle after many fun-filled attempts.

Lewin, Hugh
Jafta

Jafta depicts part of his daily feelings by likening his activity to those of several African animals.

Lewin, Hugh
Jafta's Mother

Jafta, dwelling in an African village, portrays his mother and the affection he has for her.

McKissack, Patricia
Messy Bessey

Bessey learns the importance of cleaning up and putting away her toys after play.

Steptoe, John
Baby Says

Siblings work together in a caring relationship.

Steptoe, John
Mufaro's Beautiful Daughters

The characteristics of two sisters are exposed through the acts of kindness and wickedness.

Steptoe, John
Stevie

A little boy resents sharing with others.

Williams, Vera B.
More, More, More, Said the Baby

A story of love and attention given to babies by family members.

Wilson, Beth
Jenny

In several brief lectures, Jenny shares her pleasure in the things that occupy her world.

Story Time

Lesson 1-1
Mother

Skill Areas:
Language, Cognitive, Gross Motor, Visual Motor, Fine Motor, Social

Circle Time:
Invite mothers to visit the classroom. For those children who cannot bring mothers, ask them to bring a photograph or drawing of their mother. Ask, "Whose Mom is this?" Introduce all mothers. Allow children of the mothers to present "special day" crowns to each. Involve parents in a special activity with the class.

Paint:
Have children make handprints for mothers. Print this poem for children:

> *Sometimes you get discouraged*
> *Because I am so small*
> *And always leave my fingerprints*
> *on furniture and walls.*
> *But, everyday I'm growing—*
> *I'll be grown up someday,*
> *And all these tiny fingerprints*
> *Will surely fade away.*
> *So here's a final hand print,*
> *Just so you can recall*
> *Exactly how my fingers looked*
> *When I was very small.*
> —Unknown

Creative:
Provide children with magazines showing African American women (*Ebony, Jet, Essence*), as well as women of other races. Have children cut out pictures and paste on construction paper to make a collage of mothers.

Dramatic Play:
Encourage children to "dress-up" and role-play going to a Mother's Day Tea. Provide props and clothing, for example, hats, caps, dresses, pants, wallets, purses, shoes, teacups, saucers, tea kettles, chairs, and tables.

Snack:
African Fruit Salad

Discuss with the children that a variety of fruits grow in Africa. Tell them that fruits are a significant part of the African diet. Many Africans grow fruits in their garden or buy fresh fruits from an outdoor market.

Recipe:

African Fruit Salad
(Serves 15)

2 cups pineapple chunks

2 apples

2 pears

4 ripe mangoes

1 c sugar

2 c water

1 T lemon juice

4 bananas

1 c raisins

Drain pineapple chunks and set aside in a large mixing bowl. Peel, slice, and cube apples, pears, and mangoes. Add them to the large mixing bowl. Boil sugar with water to make syrup. Allow to cool and add lemon juice. Pour syrup over fruit. Just before serving, peel and slice the bananas. Add bananas and raisins and toss.

Story:

Jafta's Mother

Finger Play:

This is my mother. (thumb)

This is my father. (pointer finger)

This is my brother tall. (middle finger)

This is my sister. (ring finger)

This is the baby. (pinkie)

Oh! How I love them all. (clap left hand over all five fingers)

—Unknown

Story:

"Ma Brown"
(Grandmother)

Once upon a time, there lived a lady named Caroline Brown. We called her "Ma Brown." Ma Brown was my grandmother. She lived in a rural community called "Browning." Many of the people who lived there had the last name Brown.

My grandmother was smart and wise! She cooked her meals on a wooden stove and sewed quilts by hand. Ma Brown always grew big gardens with lots of vegetables and fruits. She raised chickens and planted and chopped cotton every year.

Caroline Brown was also a licensed midwife. She delivered more than 5,000 babies, and she even delivered me! My grandmother at age 97 was featured in Ebony magazine in the December 1975 issue (page 116). Ma Brown lived to be 102 years of age. She was born December 25, 1878 (Christmas Day). Ma Brown—what a woman!

African American Awareness for Young Children, Copyright © 1999 Good Year Books.

Lesson 1-2
Baby

Skill Areas:
Language, Cognitive, Gross Motor, Visual Motor, Fine Motor, Social

Circle Time:
If possible, invite to class a mother who has a baby. Discuss the responsibilities parents have for their babies. Talk about importance of cleanliness and display the various items used for bathing and grooming.

Paint Area:
Precut oatmeal or grits boxes to make baby cradles. Encourage children to decorate with paint and lace.

Fine Motor:
Provide children with magazine pictures depicting African American babies. Have children paste pictures of babies and baby items on construction paper to make a collage.

Dramatic Play:
Provide baby dolls for children to bathe and dress. The water table will make an excellent bathtub.

Blocks:
Encourage children to build a playpen, using large blocks.

Snack:
Applesauce and animal crackers.

Gross Motor:
Have children crawl like a baby.

Stories:
She Come Bringing Me That Little Baby Girl
Baby Says
Everett Anderson's Nine Month Long
More, More, More, Said the Baby

Finger Play:

Baby Mark

Handsome Baby Mark
    (Lay hand in hand and move
    arms let to right.)

Dimples so deep
    (Smile.)

On his little chubby cheeks!
    (Point to cheeks.)

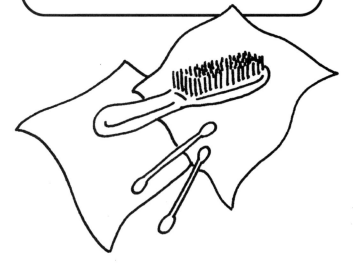

Lesson 1-3
Father

Skill Areas:

Language, Cognitive, Gross Motor, Fine Motor, Visual Motor, Social

Circle Time:

Invite fathers to visit the classroom. For those children who cannot bring fathers, ask them to bring a photograph or drawing of their father. Ask, "Whose Dad is this?" Introduce all fathers. Allow children to present "special day" crowns to each father. Involve parents in a special activity with the class.

Paint:

Provide a house shape for each child, using butcher paper and a black crayon. Each child will paint the house the color of his or her choice. Add the child's name and address to the picture.

Have children make footprints for their fathers. Print the poem "Father" for children (at right).

Creative:

Provide magazines with pictures depicting African American men (Ebony, Jet, Essence), as well as men of other races. Have children make a collage of fathers.

Dramatic Play:

Encourage the children to play "dress-up." Provide articles of men's clothing such as hats, ties, shoes, pants, and so on.

Blocks:

Provide cars, trucks, animals, and large and small blocks.

Snack:

Gingerbread cookies and milk.

Gross Motor:

Play the "Gingerbread Game." Encourage children to run and try to catch the child who is the "gingerbread man." Encourage children to say, "Run, run, as fast as you can. You can't catch me. I'm the gingerbread man." (This activity should be done outdoors or in a large area.)

Story:

Jafta

Poem:

"Father"

Father, Father,
Strong and tall!
Father, Father,
He hears my call!
Father, Father,
Always on the go!
Father, Father
I love him so!

—Dr. Mark H. Davis

African American Awareness for Young Children, Copyright © 1999 Good Year Books.

Lesson 1-4
Girl

Skill Areas:

Language, Cognitive, Gross Motor, Visual Motor, Fine Motor, Social

Circle Time:

Have children form a circle and then have all the girls in the classroom stand in front of the circle. Ask, "Who are they?" Say, "Yes, they are girls. Today will be the girls' 'special day.'" Give a head crown to each girl as she says her full name. Encourage girls to use complete sentences. For example, "My name is Nicole Titilayo Davis." Read the story *Mufaro's Beautiful Daughters*.

Fine Motor:

Provide each child with a medium-sized brown paper circle, a tongue depressor, crayons, and yarn to create a girl puppet.

Paint:

Make potato prints. "Provide pre-cut potatoes, cut out with facial features to represent a girl's face. Have each child dip the cutout face of the potato in brown paint and press it onto construction paper.

Gross Motor:

Show the children how to skip, saying "step-hop, step-hop" as you demonstrate.

Stories:

Do Like Kyla

Jenny

Messy Bessey

Snack:

Baked Yams

Yams are grown in many areas of Africa. They are a common diet staple for many African families. Let children wash yams and wrap in foil. Bake at 350° F for 1 hour. Cool and slice them, and have the boys be the servers since it is the girls' special day. Have butter, sugar, and cinnamon available so that children can experiment with different tastes for yams.

Lesson 1-5
Boy
■ ■

Skill Areas:
Language, Cognitive, Gross Motor, Visual, Fine Motor

Circle Time:
Have all the boys in the classroom stand in front of the circle. Ask, "Who are they?" Say, "Yes, they are boys. Today will be the boys' 'special day.'" Read *Jafta*. Discuss the story. Ask, "Is Jafta a boy or a girl?"

Paint:
Provide the children with an outline of a boy (such as a gingerbread-man shape). Encourage them to decorate it to look like themselves or a boy they know (if child is a girl). They can paste O-shaped cereal or fabric scraps on the boy to make facial features or clothing.

Dramatic Play:
Encourage role-play in the housekeeping area of a royal family living in Africa. Provide musical instruments such as drums, shakers, sticks, and bells. Boys play the instruments on their "special day." Play African music in the background.

Creative:
Encourage children to work together to build an African hut. Tell the children that in Africa, the walls of huts are sometimes made from red clay and the roof of the hut is oftentimes covered with palm branches. Provide grass, leaves, or straw from an old broom and tie at one end to layer the roof. Use clay to make round or square walls for the hut. Cut an opening for the door.

Finger Play:

> ### "My Royal Family"
> *This is the chief;*
> (point to pointer finger)
> *This is the queen-mother;*
> (point to middle finger)
> *This is the princess;*
> (point to the ring finger)
> *And that isn't all:*
> *Here comes the prince.*
> (point to the baby finger)
> *A very nice family*
> (raise four fingers)
> *Count them with me.*
> *1, 2, 3, 4*
> (touch each finger as you count)

Story:
Whistle for Willie

Snack:

Coconuts

In Africa, many people enjoy coconut milk as an inexpensive and readily available, refreshing drink. Bottled soda or other soft drinks are oftentimes too expensive for daily consumption by the local people. They simply chop off one end of a coconut with a machete (large knife) and drink the liquid from within. The meat on the inside also is eaten, and the shell is stockpiled for grinding into chips for other uses.

(Note: Coconuts available in the United States generally comes from Hawaii and are different in texture from the African variety. However, the children will enjoy investigating this fruit and its delicious milk and meat.)

To prepare, cover a table with plastic and use a hammer to crack open the coconut. Drain the milk out of the coconut into small cups and share with children. Scrape the insides of the coconut with a spoon and provide small portions of the coconut meat for each child to taste. Have the girls be the servers, since it is the boys' special day.

Chapter 2

Exploring the Community

This chapter on exploring the community contains seven lessons. These lessons are developed to educate and stimulate awareness in young children. This chapter will also assist children in identifying positive role models and inventions that they, at some point, may come in contact with. These inventions are visible in the everyday surroundings of young children and can easily be related to "inside/outside" school experiences. When information has been available, each lesson has biographical sketches on each person as a way of providing background information. A short synopsis is provided about each suggested story to inform the teacher ahead of time about its content. Age-appropriate stories about the inventors and their inventions are used to introduce lessons when possible. Lessons are developmentally appropriate and are based on research findings that indicate children can benefit from explicit cognitive training at a very early age. Skills are embedded into lesson activities. Pictures of the inventors and their inventions are provided as available.

OBJECTIVES

1. To develop a concept of community helpers who provide services for the community

2. To show how necessary and helpful community helpers are

3. To help children become aware of African American people who are community helpers

4. To help children develop a positive self-concept

African American Awareness for Young Children, Copyright © 1999 Good Year Books.

Clifton, Lucille
All Us Come Cross the Water

Black Americans' roots are in African countries.

Crews, Donald
School Bus

Bold pictures of common signs and symbols are illustrated in the scenery as the buses pick up children for school.

Feelings, Muriel
Jambo Means Hello: A Swahili Alphabet Book.

A Swahili alphabet book that focuses on the culture of the people

Feelings, Muriel
Mojo Means One: A Swahili Counting Book.

An East African 1 to 10 counting book written in the Swahili language

Goldin, Augusta
Straight Hair, Curly Hair

A simple description of the makeup and features of human hair

Keats, Ezra Jack
A Letter to Amy

Peter writes a letter to invite Amy to his birthday party and takes it to the mailbox in the rain.

Sarah Breedlove Walker

"Madame C. J. Walker"

1869 – 1919

Sarah Breedlove Walker, known as "Madame C. J. Walker," invented a hair softener and straightening comb. In doing so, Walker became the first African American woman to become a millionaire. She manufactured cosmetics and established beauty schools across the country. Students came from foreign countries to the United States to train in Walker's beauty schools. Walker supported many charities, organizations, and colleges. Her will specified that two-thirds of the profits of her company should be given to charitable organizations.

African American Awareness for Young Children, Copyright © 1999 Good Year Books.

Lesson 2-1
Sarah Breedlove Walker
"Madame C. J. Walker" / Straightening Comb

Skill Areas:
Language, Cognitive, Gross Motor, Visual Motor, Fine Motor, Social

Circle Time:
Introduce this lesson by reading the story *Straight Hair, Curly Hair.* Have available a straightening comb. A straightening comb is a metal comb with an attached handle. It is heated and used for pressing or straightening human hair. Discuss the usage of a straightening comb. Ask questions about opposites *(hot/cold, hard/soft)*. Tell the children that an African American woman invented the straightening comb.

Song:

> **Sarah Walker**
> Tune: "Frere Jacques"
>
> *Sarah Walker, Sarah Walker,*
> *Who was she? Who was she?*
> *She invented the straightening comb.*
> *She invented the straightening comb.*
> *Yes, she did. Yes, she did.*

Fine Motor:
Grooming Collage

- Have available department store advertisements, magazines, school catalogs, scissors, and paste. Encourage children to locate pictures of grooming supplies such as combs, hairbrushes, hair dryers, shampoo, dolls, and so on. Have them cut out the pictures and make a collage.

- Have children color the picture of Walker on p. 17. Encourage them to share the picture and their new information about Ms. Walker with their parents.

Dramatic Play:
Encourage children to groom the dolls. Bring in combs, brushes, and shampoo for the water table.

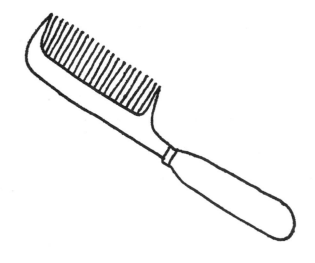

Snack:
Groundnut Cutlets
(Groundnut is an African name for peanuts.) Have children wash hands and assist in preparing the snack.

Recipe:

Groundnut Cutlets

4 oz roasted and shelled nuts
1/4 tsp salt
1/2 tsp chopped parsley
2 onions, chopped
1 tomato, chopped
1 T butter
1/2 T flour
2 oz milk
1 egg, beaten
2 T bread crumbs
1T cooking oil
1/2 lime

Mince or pound roasted nuts and set aside. Add salt and parsley to chopped onions and tomatoes. Mix into nuts. Fry in about 1 tablespoon butter. Remove ingredients from skillet and add flour. Stir in the milk to make a *panada*,* or very thick sauce for binding. Mix nut mixture with panada and then divide into four equal parts. Shape as cutlets or rolls. Brush with egg and then coat with bread crumbs. Fry in oil until golden brown. Squeeze a few drops of lime juice on cutlet before serving.

*Cooked yam, cassava, or plantain may be used instead of *panada*. Boiled beans may be used instead of roasted nuts. The mixture may be made sweet instead of savory.

Gross Motor:
Provide duplicate pictures of hair-grooming supplies and place at opposite ends of the room or yard. Encourage each child to skip from one side of the room or yard, pick up a picture, skip back, and find the matching picture.

Blocks:
Encourage children to build a beauty salon or barber shop.

Field Trip:
Plan to visit a beauty salon or barber shop in the neighborhood.

Sarah Breedlove Walker

African American Awareness for Young Children, Copyright © 1999 Good Year Books.

Name _____

Sarah Breedlove Walker, known as "Madame C. J. Walker," invented a hair softener and straightening comb. In doing so, Walker became the first African American woman to become a millionaire.

African American Awareness for Young Children, Copyright © 1999 Good Year Books.

Lyda D. Newman

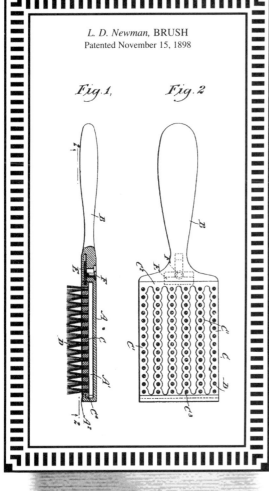

L. D. Newman, BRUSH
Patented November 15, 1898

Fig.1.   Fig.2

1 8 0 0 s

Lyda Newman invented the modern day hairbrush. She was given a patent for it on November 15, 1898. The purpose of the invention was to provide a new and improved hairbrush that was simple, durable, effective in use, and easy to clean. The hairbrush had a handle, a recess for bristles, and a side opening for ventilation and was advertised as being able to clean impurities from the scalp. Lyda Newman lived in New York City, New York, at the time of her patent. It is difficult to find personal information on Lyda.

Lesson 2-2
Lyda D. Newman
Hairbrush

Skill Areas:
Language, Visual Motor, Fine Motor, Gross Motor, Social

Circle:
Introduce this lesson by displaying a variety of hairbrushes. Discuss the shapes, sizes, and colors. Also, discuss what a hairbrush is used for. Tell the children that Lyda Newman, an African American woman, invented the hairbrush. Give each child an opportunity to match brushes according to color, then shapes, and then size. Encourage children to describe the brushes using short sentences.

Paint:
Provide children with a variety of brushes (different sizes of paintbrush, a toothbrush, etc.) for painting.

Fine Motor:
Provide the hairbrush coloring sheet on p. 21. Have children color the hairbrushes and then draw and color a picture of themselves with a new hairstyle. The style can be silly or stylish.

Gross Motor:
"Hairbrush Hop"
Divide the class into two groups. Ask for a volunteer from each group to serve as leader. Give each leader a brush. The leaders will hop on one leg to a determined point and back and then give the brush to the next person in line. The group that finishes first is the winner.

Snack:

Fried Plantain and Milk

Have children wash their hands and assist in making the snack.

Recipe:

> ### Fried Plantain
> **(serves about 15)**
>
> *2 or 3 large, ripe, yellow plantains*
> *3 c hot cooking oil*

Have available plastic knives, a large bowl, paper towels, and toothpicks. Have children peel the plantains. Teacher heats oil in skillet. Have children slice plantains into thin, round slices. Teacher places plantain slices in hot oil and fries until browned. Place fried plantains on paper towels to drain. Children can stick toothpicks into plantains to serve and eat.

Field Trip:

Department Store

Give each child an opportunity to buy a small hairbrush to take home. Discuss the selection of colors and shapes.

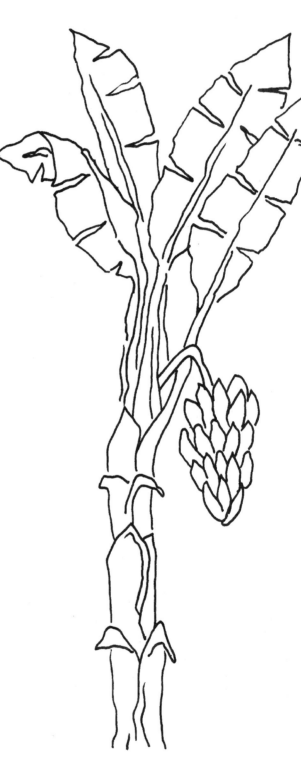

A Plantain Tree

Lyda D. Newman

Name _____

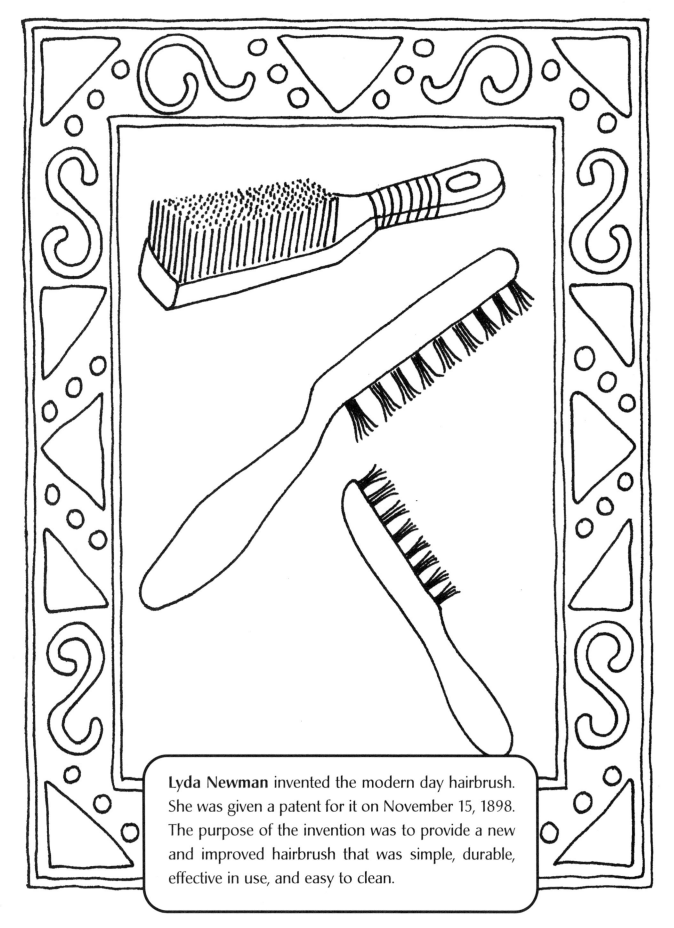

Lyda Newman invented the modern day hairbrush. She was given a patent for it on November 15, 1898. The purpose of the invention was to provide a new and improved hairbrush that was simple, durable, effective in use, and easy to clean.

Philip B. Downing

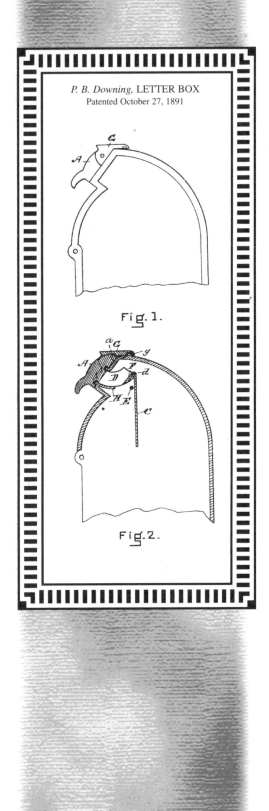

P. B. Downing, LETTER BOX
Patented October 27, 1891

Fig. 1.

Fig. 2.

P hilip B. Downing invented the mailbox. His design incorporated the hinged-door opening that is a common feature on U.S. mailboxes. The mailbox he invented consisted of a lid that covered and closed the mailing slot, a safety plate that hung vertically in the box, a transverse plate that provided a shelf for receiving the mail inside the box, a transverse strip, or weather strip, that prevented the entrance of rain or snow into the mail box, and a rod that extended from side to side for support. Philip Downing received a patent on October 27, 1891. He resided in Boston, Massachusetts, at the time of his patent. It is difficult to find biographical information on Philip.

African American Awareness for Young Children, Copyright © 1999 Good Year Books.

Lesson 2-3
Philip B. Downing
▪▪▪
Mailbox

Skill Areas:

Language, Gross Motor, Cognitive, Visual Motor, Social

Circle Time:

Show the children a large picture of a mailbox. Ask children to identify the object and tell what it is used for. Explain to the children that the mailbox was invented by an African American man, Philip Downing. Discuss the color, shape, and size of a mailbox. Tell the children that they are going to make and paint a mailbox today.

Song:

Philip Downing
Tune: "Where Is Thumbkin?"

Philip Downing,
Philip Downing,
What did he do?
What did he do?
He invented the mailbox.
He invented the mailbox.
The mail's here too!
The mail's here too!

Creative:

■ Have each child make a mailbox from a milk carton.

Cut a slot on the bottom of the carton and decorate the entire box with torn pieces of construction paper pasted to sides. If they can, have children make name and address plates on strips of light colored paper. Have them write their last names and street addresses on the side, or write the information for them, if necessary.

■ Pass out the letter format on p. 25 and ask children to write a letter to someone. Children who have trouble writing may pretend to write or write some words they know and draw a picture. Ask children to read their letters to the teacher, and ask volunteers to read to the entire class.

Dramatic Play:

Provide children with envelopes, stamps, hats, and mail bags for role-playing mail carriers.

Snack:
Cookies

Have children deliver cookies as mail to their homemade mailboxes. Wrap cookies in napkins folded like envelopes and taped closed.

Gross Motor:

Play the game "Philip Downing's Mailbox." Have children sit in a circle on the rug. One child is Philip and walks around the outer edge of the circle saying, "Philip Downing's mailbox!" When the child says *mailbox* he or she drops a homemade mailbox behind the child being tapped. The child who is tapped chases the other around the circle back to the beginning space and then walks around with the mailbox to repeat the game.

Story:

A Letter to Amy

Philip B. Downing

African American Awareness for Young Children, Copyright © 1999 Good Year Books.

Name _____

Joseph Winters

1816 –

Joseph Winters invented the fire escape ladder. His invention was given a patent on May 7, 1878. The fire escape ladder was durable, simple, inexpensive, easy to handle, and occupied little space. Also, it contained a tamper-proof alarm. Winters lived in Chambersburg, Pennsylvania, at the time of his invention. However, he was born in Leesburg, Virginia, on August 29, 1816. From 1837 through 1841 Winters owned a compilation of the *Franklin Telegraph* and *Democratic Advertiser*. Winters enjoyed fishing and spent a lot of time close to nature.

African American Awareness for Young Children, Copyright © 1999 Good Year Books.

Lesson 2-4
Joseph Winters
■ ■
Fire Escape Ladder

Skill Areas:
Language, Cognitive, Visual Motor, Gross Motor, Social

Circle Time:
Bring a small ladder to class, preferably the retractable home version specifically made for escaping from a second story window. Ask, "What is this?" Demonstrate how to use the ladder. Tell the children that an African-American man by the name of Joseph Winters invented a metal fire escape ladder—the type that is permanently attached to some buildings.

Song:

Ladder

Tune: "Did You Ever See a Lassie?"

Have you ever climbed a ladder?
A ladder? A ladder?
Have you ever climbed a ladder?
From down to up and up to down.
(Repeat.)
(Move arms up and down.)

Fine Motor:
■ Paste strips of construction paper onto vertical lines to represent rungs on a ladder.

■ Have children make a ladder from tongue depressors. Glue two parallel tongue depressors onto a piece of paper and then use crayons to draw rungs.

■ Draw a picture of a ladder, using glue and sprinkling with glitter to decorate.

■ Have children color the picture of Winters on p. 29. Encourage children to share their picture and their new information about Mr. Winters with their parents.

Dramatic Play:
Discuss fire safety and procedures and then have children pretend they are practicing a fire drill. In the drill they will need to pantomime dropping a ladder out their bedroom window and climbing down to safety. Remind children they cannot carry toys or other items with them. Let each child pantomime the drill. Suggest to children that they encourage their families to have a fire drill, so that everyone knows what to do and where to meet outside.

Snack:

Make "ladders" from popcorn and peanuts. Provide children with napkins, popcorn, and peanuts. Have children make two horizontal lines with the popcorn and four vertical lines with the peanuts.

Blocks:

Encourage children to build a fire station.

Field Trip:

Fire station

Story:

Jambo Means Hello: A Swahili Alphabet Book

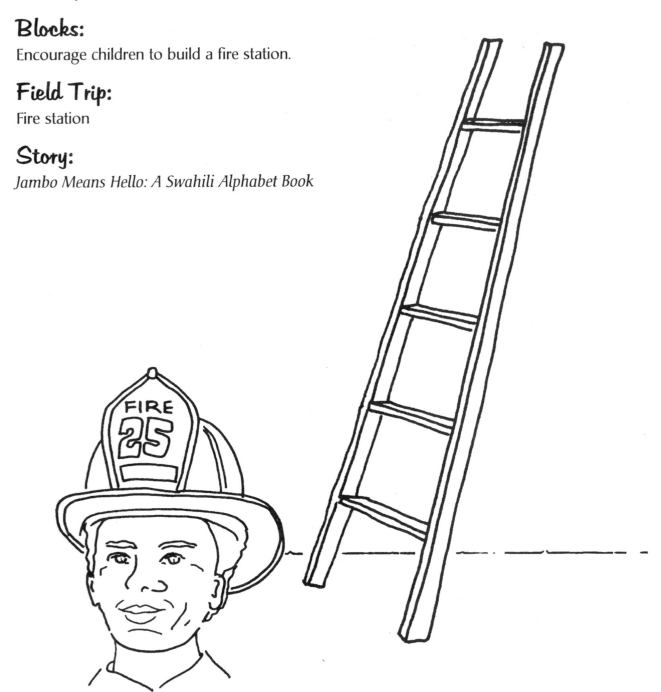

Joseph Winters

Name _____

Joseph Winters invented the fire escape ladder. His invention was given a patent on May 7, 1878. The fire escape ladder was durable, simple, inexpensive, easy to handle, and occupied little space. Also, it contained a tamper-proof alarm.

Garrett Morgan

1875 – 1963

Garrett Morgan invented devices to help save lives. One of Morgan's inventions was the automatic stop sign, better known as the traffic light. He thought of this idea after he observed an accident between an automobile and a horse and carriage. Morgan then invented the traffic light to control the flow of traffic at an intersection. Morgan also invented the gas mask (breathing mask) used by firefighters in the early 1900s. He received a gold medal from the City of Cleveland for a successful rescue operation using his gas mask invention. In 1914 he received another gold medal at the Second International Exposition of Safety and Sanitation in New York. Today, Morgan's inventions are still helping to save lives all over the world.

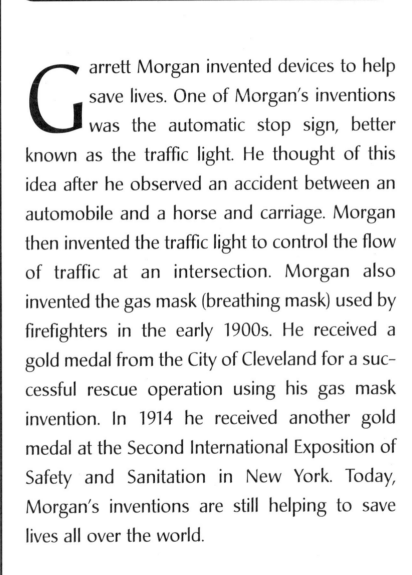

African American Awareness for Young Children., Copyright © 1999 Good Year Books.

Lesson 2-5
Garrett Morgan

▪ ▪

Traffic Light

Skill Areas:

Cognitive, Language, Visual Motor, Gross Motor, Fine Motor, Social

Circle Time:

Tell the children that Garrett Morgan, an African American, invented the traffic light. Provide a red, yellow, and green circle for each child. Review the colors and shape. Read the poem below, "Red, Yellow, Green Light." Have children repeat the poem and hold up the appropriate color.

Red, Yellow, Green Light

Red light, red light, what do you say?

I say stop and stop right away.

Yellow light, yellow light, what do you mean?

I mean wait till the light turns green.

Green light, green light, what do you say?

I say go, but first look each way.

Thank you, thank you, red, yellow, green.

Now I know what the traffic lights mean.

—John Murray

Paint Area:

▪ Have children make traffic lights by painting the inside of bottle caps. Use the colors red, yellow, and green. Glue these onto a cardboard tube.

▪ Cut three holes in a cardboard box. Have children paint the box and cover the holes with red, yellow, and green cellophane or tissue paper. Use a flashlight inside the box to make the colors light up.

Fine Motor:

Have children color the picture of Morgan on p. 33. Encourage them to share the picture and their new information about Mr. Morgan with their parents.

Snack:

Red, yellow, and green M&M's® or other small candies.

As the children eat, have them whisper *Stop*, *Wait*, or *Go* as they eat the corresponding color of candy.

Gross Motor:

Construct a traffic light on a large piece of construction paper and tape it to the floor. Give children a stack of red, yellow, and green cards. To play the game, choose a card and toss a beanbag to the same color.

Story:

School Bus

Music:

Listen to "Stop and Go" from the album *Play Your Instrument and Make a Pretty Sound* by Ella Jenkins.

Field Trip:

Walk in the neighborhood to observe a traffic light at work.

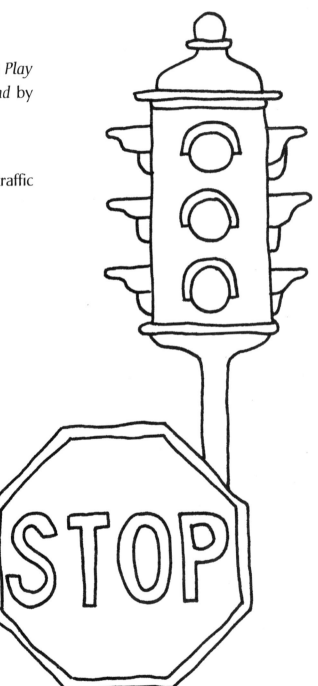

Name _____

Garrett Morgan. One of Morgan's inventions was the automatic stop sign, better known as the traffic light. He later invented the traffic light to control the flow of traffic at an intersection. Morgan also invented the gas mask (breathing mask) used by firefighters in the early 1900s Today, Morgan's inventions are still helping to save lives all over the world.

Dr. Daniel Hale Williams

1858 – 1931

In 1893 Dr. Daniel Hale Williams was the first person to perform open-heart surgery. The patient was saved when Dr. Williams performed surgery on his heart. A six-man operating team assisted Dr. Williams, who worked in a small operating room without the use of modern medical facilities, X rays, or blood transfusions. Dr. Williams opened the patient's chest, exposed the beating heart, and stitched the knife wound. Dr. Williams was also the founder of Provident Community Hospital in Chicago, Illinois.

Lesson 2-6
Dr. Daniel Hale Williams
Open-Heart Surgery

Skill Areas:
Language, Cognitive, Gross Motor, Visual Motor, Fine Motor, Social

Circle Time:
Show the children the location of the heart. Ask children to feel for their heartbeat. Tell children the heart is used to pump blood. Show the children the picture of Dr. Daniel Hale Williams. Explain that he was the first person to successfully perform open-heart surgery.

Paint Area:
Provide heart-shaped sponges for children to paint with.

Fine Motor:
- Provide an outline of a real human heart (see p. 36). Have children paste black-eyed peas, beans, macaroni, or peanuts on the outer edges.

- Have children color the picture of Dr. Williams on p. 37. Encourage them to share the picture and their new information about Dr. Williams with their parents.

Dramatic Play:
Create a doctor's office for role-playing. Provide doctor's supplies, include bandages, a blood-pressure cuff, a thermometer, and so on. Have available dolls and stuffed animals to act as patients.

Gross Motor:
Have volunteers do ten jumping jacks, checking their heart rates before and after this activity. Make a classroom line graph on chart paper. Show a blue line for "Before Jumping" and a red line for "After Jumping." Label the horizontal axis with children's names and with the vertical axis with bpm (beats per minute). Compare the two lines. See the sample graph below.

Story:
All Us Come Cross the Water

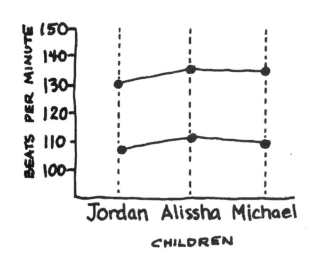

Field Trip:

Visit a doctor's office; or as an alternative, arrange for a doctor, preferably an African American one, to visit the classroom.

Snack:

Heart-Shaped Gelatin
(Serves 24)

2 large boxes (8 oz size) red gelatin dessert

heart-shaped cookie cutter or pattern cut from cardboard

2 1/2 c boiling water

13 x 9 inch flat-bottom pan

Stir powdered gelatin with boiling water until dissolved. Pour into pan and refrigerate until firm, about 3 hours. Dip bottom of pan in warm water to loosen mold. Cut gelatin into heart shapes with cookie cutter or blunt knife and then pry out with spatula. Serve.

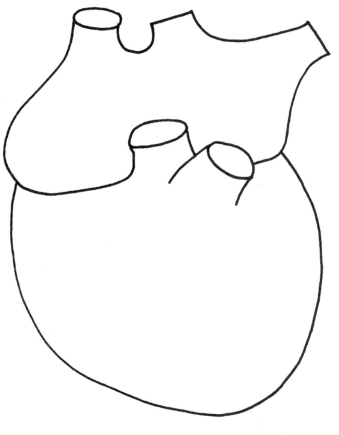

Human Heart Pattern

Dr. Daniel Hale Williams

Name _____

Dr. Daniel Hale Williams was the first person to perform open-heart surgery. A six-man operating team assisted Dr. Williams, who worked in a small operating room without the use of modern medical facilities, X rays, or blood transfusions. Dr. Williams opened the patient's chest, exposed the beating heart, and stitched the knife wound. Dr. Williams was also the founder of Provident Community Hospital in Chicago, Illinois.

Dr. Mae Jemison

1956 –

Dr. Mae Jemison was the first African American woman in space. She was accepted as a NASA astronaut in 1987, and in 1992 she was selected to fly in the space shuttle Endeavor as a mission specialist. Dr. Jemison was responsible for conducting experiments during the shuttle mission.

Jemison was born in Decatur, Alabama. She received her bachelor's degree in Chemical Engineering and Afro-American Studies from Stanford University in 1977. In 1981 she received her medical degree from Cornell University. From 1983 to 1985 she served as a medical officer for the Peace Corps in Sierra Leone and Liberia, West Africa. While there she was responsible for the health care delivery system for Peace Corps and U.S. Embassy personnel.

Lesson 2-7
Dr. Mae Jemison

Astronaut

Skill Areas:

Fine Motor, Cognitive, Language, Visual Motor, Gross Motor, Social

Circle Time:

Tell children about how the space program helps us learn about our Earth. Tell them that spaceships have traveled around the Earth and have taken people to the moon. Also tell them that there have been spaceships without people in them that have landed on Mars and have traveled deep within our solar system, taking photographs.

Introduce this action poem and the following song.

Mae Jemison

Mae Jemison
Inside a rocketship,
       (squatting position)
She is an astronaut
Ready to take off.
       (Rise slowly.)
1-2-3-4-5- Blast Off!
       (Extend arms toward sky.)
Up, up, up.
       (Jump three times.)

The Endeavor
Tune: "Good Morning"

Endeavor!
Endeavor!
The name of the Ship!

       (repeat verse twice)

Endeavor!
Endeavor!
That took Jemison up!
That took Jemison up!
That took Jemison up!

Have available pictures of spacesuits, helmets, rocket ships, and astronauts. Tell the children that an astronaut is a person who is trained to fly a spacecraft. Give the children an opportunity to discuss and ask questions. Provide toy objects for hands-on experience. Ask the children to say the name "Mae Jemison." Tell them that she is the first African American female astronaut. Show a picture of Jemison dressed in her spacesuit, p. 38.

Fine Motor:

- Provide supplies to assist children in constructing a space rocket. Provide shapes such as triangles, crescents, and stars to cut, paste, and color. Have them paste the shapes on empty paper-towel or toilet-paper rolls.

- Have children color the picture of Jemison on p. 41. Encourage them to share the picture and their new information about Dr. Jemison with their parents.

Paints:

Show children a picture of our solar system. Tell them the names of the planets, as well as a common mnemonic device to help them memorize the order (My Very Educated Mother Just Served Us Nice Pie). Have them paint a solar system on a blank sheet of paper, making sure to include the sun and the nine planets. Those who can should label their planets.

Blocks:

Encourage children to build a launching pad (an area or structure from which a rocket is launched). First, have children construct a large, square shape out of blocks. Then build a medium-sized triangle out of blocks inside of the square. Make four balls out of newspaper and cover with foil. Place balls in each corner of the square to represent landing lights. Children can use rocket ships made in the Fine Motor activity for launching from the launching pad.

Gross Motor/Dramatic Play:

Encourage children to walk as if they were on the moon. Demonstrate light and slow movements.

Song:

Listen to "I Believe I Can Fly" by R. Kelly on the *Space Jam Motion Picture Soundtrack.*

Snack:

Moon Pie® and Milk

A Moon Pie is a large sandwich cookie with marshmallow filling and a flavored coating. Learn about moon pies on the Moon Pie home page at ***http://moonpie.com.***

Field Trip:

If possible, visit a local airport to observe airplanes landing and taking off. As an alternative, visit your local library at story time. Request stories about space.

Story:

Mojo Means One: A Swahili Counting Book

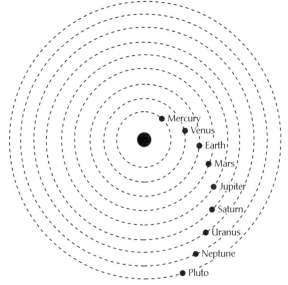

Dr. Mae Jemison

African American Awareness for Young Children, Copyright © 1999 Good Year Books.

Dr. Mae Jemison was the first African American woman in space. She was accepted as a NASA astronaut in 1987, and in 1992 she was selected to fly in the space shuttle Endeavor as a mission specialist. Dr. Jemison was responsible for conducting experiments during the shuttle mission.

Social Interaction

This chapter on social interaction contains six complete lessons centered around famous African Americans and their contributions to society. These lessons focus on positive role models, personal relationships, manners, common courtesy, self-concept, and the ability to resolve conflicts without violence. The lessons include biographical sketches on each person. On the Story Time page, a short synopsis is provided about each suggested story. Coloring sheets are provided with each lesson.

OBJECTIVES

1. To help children become aware that people of African American heritage have made important contributions in America

2. To foster an awareness of our common humanity

3. To help children develop positive self-concepts

African American Awareness for Young Children, Copyright © 1999 Good Year Books.

Benjamin, Ann
Young Rosa Parks

A biography of Rosa Parks growing up and working for civil rights

Crews, Donald
School Bus

Bold pictures of common signs and symbols are illustrated as buses pick up children for school.

Farrell, Edward
Young Jackie Robinson

An easy-to-read biography of the first black baseball player to play for a Major League team.

Greenfield, Eloise
Me and Nessie

A story of a little girl and her imaginary friend

Hudson, Cheryl W., and Bernette G. Ford
Bright Eyes, Brown Skin

Positive attributes of African American children

Isadora, Rachel
Friends

A picture book of multiracial children playing together

Story Time

▪ ▪ ▪ ▪ ▪ ▪ ▪ ▪ ▪ ▪ ▪ ▪ ▪ ▪ ▪ ▪ ▪

James, Cynthia
The Gifts of Kwanzaa

The Kwanzaa celebration explained in simple terms

Kurtz, Jane
I'm Calling Molly

A young boy learns to use the telephone and calls a playmate.

Mattern, Jeanne
Young Martin Luther King, Jr.: I Have a Dream

A biography of the great civil rights leader, minister, and winner of the Nobel Peace Prize

McKissack, Patricia
Nettie Jo's Friends

Nettie Jo's friends seem reluctant to help her find a needle to sew her doll's dress.

Myers, Walter D.
Young Martin's Promise

Unfair laws and racism separate and sadden children.

Newton, Deborah
My First Kwanzaa Books

Introduces an African American cultural celebration

Udry, Janice
What Mary Jo Shared

Mary Jo wants to bring something unique for Show and Tell.

Dr. Martin Luther King, Jr.

1929 – 1968

Dr. Martin Luther King, Jr., was a minister, civil rights leader, and recipient of the Nobel Peace Prize. King believed in equal rights and worked very hard for the benefit of African Americans. He said that all people should be treated equally and with respect. When the Montgomery Improvement Association (Montgomery, Alabama) was organized in 1955 because of unfair laws, King was elected president. He led the bus boycott against the Municipal Bus Company that was instrumental in creating the Civil Rights Act of the 1960s. King received two undergraduate degrees from Boston University as well as a doctoral degree in Systematic Theology. He was also awarded honorary degrees from many colleges and universities in the United States and abroad. Nine years after his death, the United States honored him with the Congressional Medal of Freedom and declared his birthday a national holiday.

Lesson 3-1
Dr. Martin Luther King, Jr.
Nonviolence

Skill Areas:
Gross Motor, Fine Motor, Cognitive, Language

Circle:
Read the book *Young Martin Luther King, Jr: I Have a Dream*. Discuss that King believed all children should be allowed to play together and become friends.

Paint:
Provide children with a large rectangular sheet of posterboard; sponge alphabet letters; and red, black, and green paint. Use sponge alphabet letters to make the sign "Martin Luther King Jr. Drive." Hang finished projects in the classroom.

Fine Motor:
- Trace each child's body on butcher paper. Provide crayons, yarn (hair), and black-eyed peas (eyes) for decorations. Align the pictures on the wall of the classroom as if hand and hand in peace. If you have space constraints, consider making the outlines smaller than life-size.

- Have children color the picture of King on p. 47. Encourage them to share the picture and their new information about King with their parents.

Blocks:
Have children build a street to represent Martin Luther King Jr. Drive. Give children toy cars or something representing cars to take turns with for driving on this street. Encourage them to make car noises. This activity provides children with an opportunity for self-expression, nonviolent emotional release, and use of gross and fine motor skills.

Gross Motor:
Provide musical instruments, and allow children to hold a march for peace. In their march for peace, children should walk from one point to another carrying banners or chanting words that stress the concept of living in harmony with others. Provide teacher-made banners or have children assist in creating them.

Stories:
Young Martin Luther King, Jr.: I Have a Dream
Young Martin's Promise

Song:

> ### Who Was Martin Luther King?
> Tune: "Old MacDonald"
>
> *Who was Martin Luther King?*
> *The man who had a dream.*
> *Let's all join hands in harmony*
> *That's what made us free.*
>
> ### Chorus
> Tune: "Bingo" (chorus)
>
> *Mar-tin Luther King*
> *Mar-tin Luther King*
> *Mar-tin Luther King*
> *The man who had a dream*
> *YEAH!*
>
> —Dr. Mark H. Davis

Field Trip:

Martin Luther King Jr. Drive

If possible take children to see any street named in King's honor and take a picture of the road sign with children around it. Display the photo in the classroom. If not possible, plan a special program honoring King. Invite a guest speaker to talk about King's life and mission and invite parents as guests.

Snack:

African Rice Bread

African rice bread is common in West Africa. Africans usually eat large meals at noon and in the evening. However, they snack most of the day on foods such as rice bread. Rice is an important part of the African diet. Have children wash hands and assist in preparing this snack. Provide cooking utensils. You will need two mixing bowls, measuring cups, spoons, a fork, a knife, a potato masher, a 9 x 5 x 3 inch loaf pan, paper plates, and napkins.

Recipe:

> ### African Rice Bread
> (Serves 16)
>
> *1 c cooked rice*
> *3 T melted butter*
> *1 egg yolk*
> *1 banana, mashed*
> *1 c milk*
> *1/2 tsp salt*
> *1 tsp nutmeg*
> *2 tsp baking powder*
> *3 T sugar*

Grease pan and preheat oven to 375°F. Mix hot cooked rice and melted butter. In a separate bowl, beat egg yolk, add mashed banana and milk, and stir in dry ingredients. Combine with rice and butter. Put into a loaf pan and form into a loaf. Bake for 45 minutes. Cool and serve.

African American Awareness for Young Children, Copyright © 1999 Good Year Books.

Name _____

Dr. Martin Luther King, Jr., was a minister, civil rights leader, and recipient of the Nobel Peace Prize. King believed in equal rights and worked very hard for the benefit of African Americans. He said that all people should be treated equally and with respect. Nine years after his death, the United States honored him with the Congressional Medal of Freedom and declared his birthday a national holiday.

Lesson 3-2
Dr. Martin Luther King, Jr.
Friendship

Skill Areas:

Language, Cognitive, Gross Motor, Visual Motor, Fine Motor, Social

Circle Time:

Read the book *Friends* by Rachel Isadora. Discuss the story in detail. Ask, "Do you have a friend?" Explain that a friend is a person that you can share with, talk to, and play with. Tell the children that today they are going to have a Friendship Day. Encourage sharing and playing together in pairs. If possible, read children Martin Luther King, Jr's, I Have a Dream speech on p. 50, or at least an excerpt, and discuss what he meant.

Paint:

Encourage children to share, work together, and make a "friendship" train. Use the pattern on p. 51 to provide precut rectangles and circles from white construction paper. Provide one long sheet of butcher paper, yarn, paint, paint brushes, and glue. Have children glue the shapes onto the paper, forming box cars, a caboose, and wheels. Teacher can cut out and paint the engine. Use yarn to connect the cars. Have children write their names with marker on the friendship train, or assist them in doing so. Have children color and then hang finished project in classroom.

Creative:

Encourage children to make friendship bracelets. Provide shoelaces and beads for each child to string. Encourage children to use red beads (representing continuing struggle), black beads (symbolizing the color of African people), and green beads (representing the Motherland, Africa).

Blocks:

Have children build something with a friend.

Gross Motor:

Have relay races and discuss group cooperation.

Stories:

Friends
Me and Nessie
Nettie Jo's Friends

African American Awareness for Young Children, Copyright © 1999 Good Year Books.

Rhyme:

Have children sit in a circle and each take a turn saying the rhyme, using the name of the child to their right as the "friend" name. Continue around the circle clockwise.

Friends

My friend is with me in every way.

My friend helps me through the day.

My friend calls me on the telephone.

My friend will never leave me on my own.

My friend, of course, is _____!

—Mark H. Davis II

Dramatic Play:

Provide props for children to role-play and recite an excerpt from King's famous I Have A Dream speech.

Snack:

Homemade Lemonade

Lemonade is a cool, refreshing drink made with sugar, water, and lemons. A lemon has a thick, yellow rind and an oval shape with sour juice inside. Discuss vocabulary words such as *sweet* and *sour*. Encourage children to taste juice before sugar is added. Poll the children to ascertain which taste is preferred.

Recipe:

Homemade Lemonade
(Serves 16)

12 c of water

12 large lemons

1 1/4 c sugar

Have lemons and then use a lemon squeezer to extract the lemon juice. Show the children a lemon squeezer and let them help. Grate 1 tablespoon's worth of rind. Heat sugar and water on low heat until the sugar dissolves. Mix in lemon juice and rind, and put lemonade into the refrigerator to chill.

Dr. Martin Luther King, Jr.

Dr. Martin Luther King, Jr.

Following is an excerpt of the famous speech given by Martin Luther King, Jr. on Aug. 28, 1963, at the Lincoln Memorial in Washington, D.C.

– I Have a Dream –

I say to you today, my friends, so even though we face the difficulties of today and tomorrow, I still have a dream. It is a dream deeply rooted in the American dream.

I have a dream that one day this nation will rise up and live out the true meaning of its creed: "We hold these truths to be self-evident; that all men are created equal." I have a dream that one day on the red hills of Georgia the sons of former slaves and sons of former slaveowners will be able to sit down together at the table of brotherhood.

I have a dream that my four children will one day live in a nation where they will not be judged by the color of their skin but by the content of their character.

This is our hope. This is the faith that I go back to the South with. With this faith we will be able to hew out of the mountain of despair a stone of hope. With this faith we will be able to transform the jangling discords of our nation into a beautiful symphony of brotherhood.

With this faith we will be able to work together, to pray together, to struggle together, to go to jail together, to stand up for freedom together, knowing that we will be free one day.

And this will be the day. This will be the day when all of God's children will be able to sing with new meaning, "My country 'tis of thee, sweet land of liberty, of thee I sing. Land where my fathers died, land of the Pilgrims' pride, from every mountainside, let freedom ring."

Let freedom ring from the snowcapped Rockies of Colorado! Let freedom ring from the curvaceous slopes of California! But not only that; let freedom ring from Stone Mountain of Georgia! Let freedom ring from Lookout Mountain of Tennessee! Let freedom ring from every hill and every molehill of Mississippi. From every mountainside, let freedom ring.

And when this happens, and when we allow freedom to ring, when we let it ring from every village and every hamlet, from every state and every city, we will be able to speed up that day when all of God's children, black men and white men, Jews and Gentiles, Protestants and Catholics, will be able to join hands and sing in the words of the old Negro spiritual, "Free at last! Free at last! Thank God Almighty, we are free at last!"

African American Awareness for Young Children, Copyright © 1999 Good Year Books.

Pattern: Boxcars and Wheels

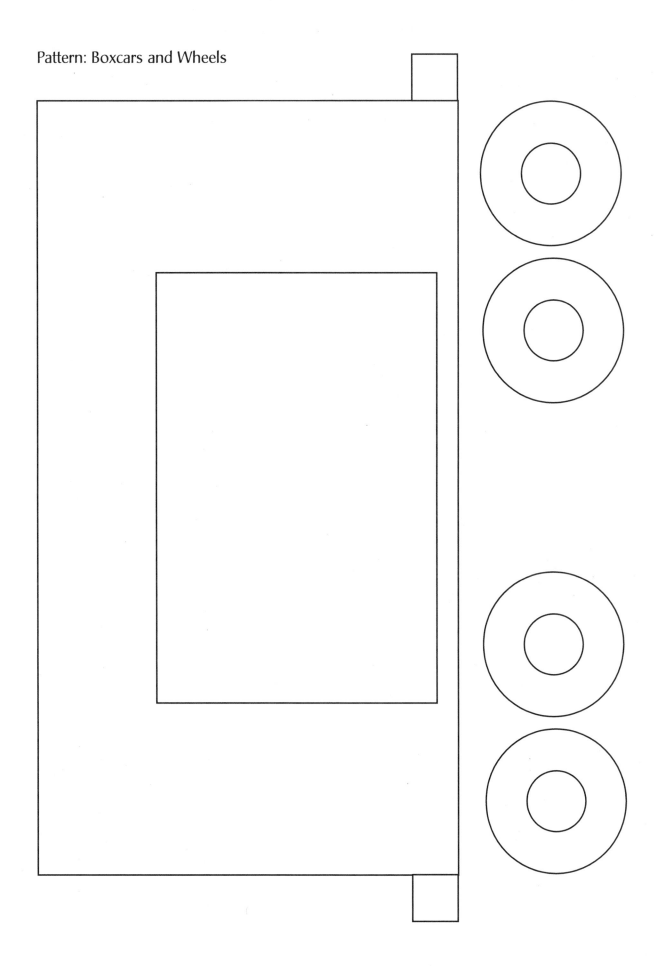

Dr. Maulana Karenga

1900s

Dr. Maulana Karenga created Kwanzaa in 1966. Kwanzaa is a festival celebrated by African Americans, but it is gradually gaining acknowledgment and importance in other parts of the world. The word *Kwanzaa* means "first fruits" (referring to first fruits of the harvest). It is through this celebration that traditional African principles are taught or reinforced. The ultimate aim of Kwanzaa is to strengthen family values.

Karenga is an internationally recognized authority in African and African American studies and is the recipient of many awards for his leadership role in the community. When this book was written, he was a professor and chairman of Black Studies at California State University at Long Beach, and the executive director of the Institute of Pan-African Studies.

Many notable works have been written by Karenga, including *The African American Holiday of Kwanzaa*, published by University of Sankore Press.

Lesson 3-3
Dr. Maulana Karenga
Kwanzaa

Skill Area:
Gross Motor, Fine Motor, Cognitive, Social, Language

Circle:
Tell children that *Kwanzaa* means "first fruits." Have available a bowl of fruits, such as grapes, pears, and apples. Have children name each fruit. Tell them that Dr. Karenga, an African American man, created this holiday. Let them know that this cultural celebration is observed from December 26 through January 1. Show children those dates on the calendar relative to today's date.

Creative:
- Have children cut out fruits and vegetables from grocery-store advertisements and create a collage to represent "first fruits." Paste pictures on paper plates.

- Provide red, black, and green construction paper. Encourage each child to create a *mkeka* (placemat). Mkekas are decorated to symbolize the history and tradition of African American people. Provide children with magazines so they can cut out and paste on their mkekas examples of things that are important to them.

- Create a necklace using O-shaped cereal, beads, or mostaccioli noodles. Children can give these as gifts *(zawadi)* to parents. Mix three drops of food coloring and one cup of water to create a dye for the noodles.

Fine Motor:
- Provide the children with the outline of a kinara (candleholder) and candles (see p. 54). Encourage children to color the kinara using red (to represent continuing struggle), black (to symbolize the color of African people), and green (to represent the Motherland, Africa).

- Have available black-eyed peas and glue for forming letters. Encourage each child to assist in tracing the seven principles of Kwanzaa. Realistically, you should provide one a day in sequential order.

- Have children color the picture of Karenga on p. 55. Encourage them to share the picture and their new information about Dr. Karenga with their parents.

Paint:
Encourage children to place hands in red, black, or green paint and then place their hand prints on paper. The fingers become candles. Help the children to make a "flame" for each candle by using a fingertip.

Seven Principles

1. *Umoja* (oo–MOH–jah) means "unity."

2. *Kujichagulia* (koo–jee–chah–goo–LEE–ah) means "self-determination."

3. *Ujima* (oo–JEE–mah) means "collective work and responsibility."

4. *Ujamaa* (oo–jah–MAH–ah) means "cooperative economics."

5. *Nia* (NEE–ah) means "purpose."

6. *Kuumba* (Koo–OOM–bah) means "creativity."

7. *Imani* (ee–MAH–nee) means "faith."

Stories:
The Gift of Kwanzaa
My First Kwanzaa

Snack:
Watermelon (sliced)
Watermelons are one of many foods that grow on vines. They are widely grown in Africa. Watermelons come in many shapes, sizes, and colors. Inside their rind is a sweet, juicy, and delicious treat.

Filmstrip:
Kwanzaa: A New Afro-American Holiday (20364–OLT)

Show this *Kwanzaa* filmstrip, which analyzes the celebration's seven principles.

Source: SVE and Church Hill Media
           6677 N. Northwest Highway
           Chicago, IL 60631
Phone: (773) 775-9550

Dr. Maulana Karenga

Name _____

Dr. Maulana Karenga created Kwanzaa in 1966. Kwanzaa is a festival celebrated by African Americans, but it is gradually gaining acknowledgment and importance in other parts of the world. The word *Kwanzaa* means "first fruits" (referring to first fruits of the harvest). It is through this celebration that traditional African principles are taught or reinforced. The ultimate aim of Kwanzaa is to strengthen family values.

Rosa Parks

1913 –

Rosa Parks is known as the "mother of the Civil Rights movement." She was arrested, fingerprinted, jailed, and fined $14.00 in 1955 in Montgomery, Alabama, because she refused to give up her seat on a city bus to a white man. The bus company policy was that the first ten seats were reserved for whites, even if the seats were not filled. A boycott was formed against the municipal bus company by the city's African American community. This was one of the first protests leading to the Civil Rights Act of 1964. Parks's courageous stance made it possible for African Americans to sit in any available seat on a bus intended for public transport.

African American Awareness for Young Children, Copyright © 1999 Good Year Books.

Lesson 3-4
Rosa Parks

Self-Concept

Skill Areas:

Language, Cognitive, Gross Motor, Visual Motor, Fine Motor, Social

Circle Time:

Read *Bright Eyes, Brown Skin.* Discuss the story in detail (race, hair, skin, eyes, etc.).

Paint Area:

Have children make hand and foot prints. Compare and note differences. Discuss the fact that no two prints are alike.

Fine Motor:

- Encourage children to create a drawing of themselves. Discuss parts and shapes of the body. Provide children with an array of skin colors. (Crayola® makes multicultural skin color crayons.) Use crayons for skin, yarn for hair, and black-eyed peas or buttons for eyes.

- Have children color the picture of Parks on p. 59. Encourage them to share the picture and their new information about Ms. Parks with their parents.

Dramatic Play:

Encourage children to role-play getting on and off a city bus. Review good manners, such as waiting your turn in line, not pushing, taking up only one seat, not eating or drinking, being quiet, and thanking the bus driver when leaving. You may also want to suggest that students give up their seats to older riders, the disabled, or pregnant women. This is also an excellent opportunity to discuss bus safety.

Blocks:

Encourage children to build a bus station. Promote positive social interaction by encouraging children to share in the construction process.

Gross Motor:

Have children practice balancing on one foot for 5–10 seconds, as if they are standing on a bus that is turning sharp corners.

Snack:

Fufu

Fufu is a very tasty Ghanaian dish. In Ghana, West Africa, fufu is made with cassava (which tapioca is made from) or sweet potatoes or yams. It is served with soup or as a side dish.

Have children wash hands and assist in preparing snack.

Recipe:

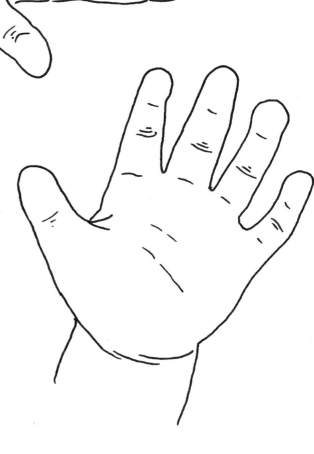

> ### Fufu
> **(Makes 24 balls)**
>
> *2 lb sweet potatoes*
> *12 cups water*
> *2 tsp ground nutmeg*
> *1 tsp ground red pepper*
> *2 T sugar*

Provide a mixing bowl, measuring cup, spoon, potato masher, large pot with lid, and napkins. Put sweet potatoes in pot with water and bring to a boil. Reduce heat and simmer for 45 minutes or until done. Remove from heat, cool, peel, and cut into small chunks and then mash until smooth. Add nutmeg, pepper, and sugar. Have children moisten hands and roll mixture into small balls. Serve.

Rosa Parks is known as the "mother of the Civil Rights movement." She was arrested, fingerprinted, jailed, and fined $14.00 in 1955 in Montgomery, Alabama, because she refused to give up her seat on a city bus to a white man. Parks's courageous stance made it possible for African Americans to sit in any available seat on a bus intended for public transport.

Lewis Howard Latimer

1 8 4 8 – 1 9 2 8

Lewis Howard Latimer, who was a patent expert, a draftsman, and an inventor, made the first drawing of the telephone. However, the telephone was patented in 1876 by Alexander Graham Bell. In 1881, Latimer invented and patented a method of making carbon filaments for Edison's lightbulb. Carbon filaments helped to increase the life of the bulb.

Latimer worked and made patents for Maxim Weston (Westinghouse) and Edison Electric (General Electric) Companies. In 1892 the companies merged and selected Latimer to serve as the chief draftsman.

Lewis Howard Latimer

Lesson 3-5
Lewis Howard Latimer
Telephone (First Drawing)

Skill Areas:
Language, Cognitive, Visual, Gross Motor, Fine Motor, Social,

Circle Time:
Show the children a picture of a play telephone. Explain to children that an African American man named Lewis Latimer provided the first drawing for the telephone. Provide a play phone and demonstrate how to dial and answer a telephone. Give each child an opportunity to dial his or her phone number.

Paint Area:
Give the children an opportunity to make a phone booth from a large box. Encourage all children to help paint the box.

Fine Motor:
- Provide a cutout drawing of a telephone for each child, (see the outline on p. 62). Print his or her name and phone number on it. Trace over the numbers with glue. Have children sprinkle sand on the glue. Use this activity to learn phone numbers. Encourage children to trace over numbers with fingers.
- Have children color the picture of Latimer on p. 63. Encourage children to share the picture and their new information about Latimer with their parents.

Gross Motor:
Set up an obstacle course that will require children to skip and crawl around toy telephones or pictures of telephones drawn on something sturdy, such as shoe boxes.

Finger Play:

Telephones

Three bright telephones;
    (Hold up three fingers.)
Red, yellow, and green.
Laurel took the red one,
    (Bend down pointer finger.)
Then there were two.

Two bright telephones;
    (Hold up two fingers.)
Yellow and green.
Claudine took the yellow phone,
    (Bend down the middle finger.)
Then there was one.

One green telephone all alone.
    (Hold up one finger.)
Jeanette took it,
Then there was none.
    (Make fist with hand.)
What's a number for none?
Zero!
    (Draw a circle in the air.)

Stories:

What Mary Jo Shared

I'm Calling Molly

Snack:

Fish Sticks

(Needed: frozen fish sticks and microwave, electric skillet, or oven)

Many of the people in coastal Africa earn a living by fishing. They get up early in the morning and leave the shore in canoes or boats. They paddle the canoes far out into the ocean and spend the day. Upon returning, their canoes are loaded with fish. They smoke, or cook, the fish in outdoor ovens and sell what they don't eat.

Lewis Howard Latimer, who was a patent expert, a draftsman, and an inventor, made the first drawing of the telephone. However, the telephone was patented in 1876 by Alexander Graham Bell. In 1881, Latimer invented and patented a method of making carbon filaments for Edison's lightbulb. Latimer worked and made patents for Maxim Weston (Westinghouse) and Edison Electric (General Electric) Companies.

Jackie Robinson

1919 – 1972

Jackie Robinson, in 1947, was the first African American to play for a Major League baseball team, the Brooklyn Dodgers. He was named Rookie of the Year that year and two years later was designated the National League's Most Valuable Player. In 1962, Robinson became the first African American to be inducted into the Baseball Hall of Fame. During his career, Robinson contributed to the Dodgers winning six National League pennants and one World Championship. Robinson's career batting average was .311 in 1,382 games. He had a total of 1,518 hits, 947 runs, 237 doubles, and 734 RBIs.

Robinson was born in Cairo, Georgia, on January 31, 1919, and grew up in Pasadena, California. On October 24, 1972, he died in Stamford, Connecticut, at the age of 53. Jackie Robinson was more than a good baseball player... he was GREAT!

African American Awareness for Young Children, Copyright © 1999 Good Year Books.

Lesson 3-6
Jackie Robinson

Baseball

Skill Areas:
Language, Gross Motor, Visual, Cognitive, Fine Motor, Social

Circle:
Introduce children to Jackie Robinson, famous African American. Tell children that he was the first African American to play professional baseball for a major league team, the Brooklyn Dodgers. Present a baseball and ask: "What is this?", "What do we use a baseball for?", "What goes with a baseball?" Show baseball pictures or objects such as a bat, glove, cap, and so on. Give children an opportunity to touch, identify, and examine each object. If possible, bring in some baseball cards to show.

Paint:
Have children do sponge paintings using diamond, square, and circle shapes. Tell them that a baseball field has these shapes: the infield diamond, square bases, and round pitcher's mound.

Fine Motor:
- Make a baseball field using tongue depressors.

- Cut triangles from construction paper to make pennants with team names. Have children paste triangles on tongue depressors.

- Color the picture of Robinson on p. 67. Encourage children to share the picture and their new information about Mr. Robinson with their parents.

Blocks:
Encourage children to build a baseball field using blocks.

Dramatic Play:
- Provide baseball clothing for children to dress-up. Have available uniforms, gloves, caps, plastic bats, and balls.

- Have children pretend they are real players and role-play playing a game without props. Pantomime pitching, batting, catching, fielding, umpires making calls, fans cheering, running bases, and so on.

Snack:
Popcorn and Peanuts

Story:

Young Jackie Robinson

Rhyme:

Jackie Robinson Baseball

Baseball! Baseball!
Jackie played the game!
Baseball! Baseball!
He made the Hall of Fame!

—Mark H. Davis II

Music:

Teach children the song, "Take Me Out to the Ball Game"

Take Me Out to the Ball Game

Take me out to the ball game.

Take me out to the crowd.

Buy me some peanuts and Crackerjacks.

I don't care if I ever get back.

Oh it's root, root, root, for the home team.

If they don't win it's a shame.

For it's one, two, three strikes you're out at the old ball game.

Field Trip:

Take the children to a real game or visit the dugout of any baseball field. If neither is possible, consider showing the class one inning of a baseball game on TV or "assigning" students to watch one at home.

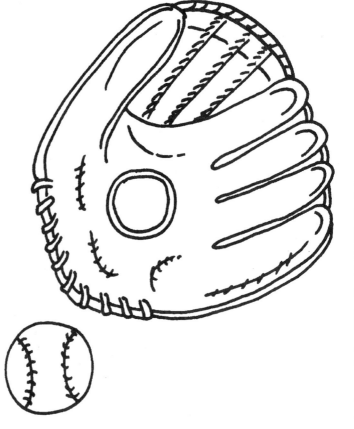

Jackie Robinson, in 1947, was the first African American to play for a Major League baseball team, the Brooklyn Dodgers. He was named Rookie of the Year that year and two years later was designated the National League's Most Valuable Player. In 1962, Robinson became the first African American to be inducted into the Baseball Hall of Fame. Jackie Robinson was more than a good baseball player... he was GREAT!

African American Inventors

This chapter on African American inventors contains five complete lessons centered around the inventors and their creations. These inventions are in the everyday surroundings of young children. The lessons include biographical sketches on each person, when available, as a way of providing background information and an explanation of the item invented. On the Story Time page, a short synopsis is provided about each suggested story. Age-appropriate stories about the inventors and their inventions are used to introduce the lesson when available. Lessons are developmentally appropriate and are based on research findings that indicate children can benefit from explicit cognitive training at a very early age. Skills are embedded into lesson activities. Pictures of the inventors/inventions, patterns, and coloring and drawing sheets are provided with each lesson.

OBJECTIVES

1. To model the African American culture as vibrant and positive

2. To develop an awareness of the advances and contributions that African Americans have made in various occupational fields

3. To help children develop a positive self-concept

Story Time

Aliki
A Weed Is a Flower: The Life of George Washington Carver

Describes the life of a former slave who became a scientist and devoted his career to helping others

Freeman, Don
A Pocket for Corduroy

An adventure of Lisa and her teddy bear

Goldin, Augusta
Straight Hair, Curly Hair

A simple description of the makeup and features of human hair

McKissack, Patricia
Flossie and the Fox

The tale of a courageous little girl and a slick fox

Mitchell, Barbara
A Pocketful of Goobers: A Story About George Washington Carver

A biography of George Washington Carver and the products he invented from peanuts, soybeans, and sweet potatoes

Patrick, Denise
Red Dancing Shoes

A young girl receives a special pair of red dancing shoes that make her feet feel magical.

George Washington Carver

1864 – 1943

George Washington Carver was a plant scientist who made great contributions to the field of agricultural chemistry. He created more than three hundred products from peanuts, soybeans, and sweet potatoes. He received his master's degree from Iowa State University and was the first African American to serve on the university's faculty. It was at Tuskegee Institute, where Carver was employed as an agricultural scientist, that he came up with his plant-rotation ideas. By planting clover, peas, and peanuts on a rotating basis, farmers could restore nutrients back into the soil. Carver received many honors and awards for his work. Many institutions, museums, and schools are named in honor of George Washington Carver.

Lesson 4-1
George Washington Carver
Peanuts

Skill Areas:
Language, Cognitive, Gross Motor, Visual, Fine Motor, Social

Circle:
Introduce the children to a famous African American inventor, George Washington Carver. Help children discover that he invented peanut butter and other products using peanuts. Explain to the children that the peanut comes from Africa and is sometimes called a *goober*. Read to children *A Pocketful of Goobers*.

Tell children about other products Carver made from the peanut or sweet potato, such as, milk, soap, cheese, instant coffee, flour, starch, and ink.

Paint:
Sponge Painting—Provide a sponge the shape of a peanut, brown paint, and construction paper. See Appendix, p. 105, for possible places to purchase the sponge, or use the pattern on p. 73.

Fine Motor:
■ Have children color the picture of George Washington Carver on p. 75. Encourage them to share the picture and their new information about Mr. Carver with their parents.

■ Provide the peanut vine pattern on p. 74. Have children paste real peanuts on the vine and use green crayons to color the leaves.

Snack:
Peanut butter and jelly sandwiches

Gross Motor:

Have children do the actions as they sing the song "Peanut Butter."

Peanut Butter

Chorus:

Peanut, peanut butter–jelly

Peanut, peanut butter–jelly

Verse 1:

First you take the nuts and you crack them, you crack them, you crack them, crack them, crack them.

Then you take the nuts and you mash them,

you mash them, you mash them, mash them, mash them.

Then you take the nuts and you stir them, you stir them, you stir them, stir them, stir them.

(Repeat chorus.)

Verse 2:

Then you take the berries and you pick them, you pick them, you pick them, pick them, pick them. Then you take the berries and you squash them, you squash them, you squash them, squash them, squash them.

(Repeat chorus.)

Verse 3:

Then you take the peanut butter, and you take a big slice of bread, and you spread it, you spread it, you spread it, spread it, spread it.

Then you take the jelly and you spread it, you spread it, you spread it, spread it, spread it.

Now you take a big sandwich and you bite it, you bite it, you bite, bite it, bite it.

Then you chew it, you chew it, you chew it, chew it, chew it. (Repeat chorus with "mmmm.")

Now you take the big glass of milk and you drink it, you drink it, you drink it, drink it, drink it.

Now you gulp it, you gulp it, you gulp it (gulp) (gulp).

Wasn't that good? mmmm!

(Repeat chorus twice.)

—Traditional

Science:

Provide sweet potatoes for children. Have them root sweet potatoes plants in a container of water.

Story:

A Weed Is a Flower: The Life of George Washington Carver

Pattern: Peanut

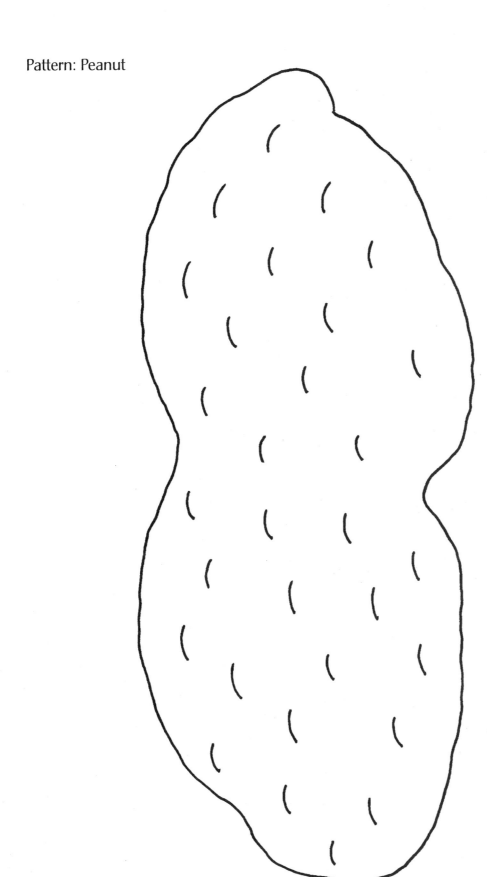

Pattern: Peanut Vine

George Washington Carver

George Washington Carver was a plant scientist who made great contributions to the field of agricultural chemistry. He created more than three hundred products from peanuts, soybeans, and sweet potatoes. Carver received many honors and awards for his work. Many institutions, museums, and schools are named in honor of George Washington Carver.

Sarah Boone

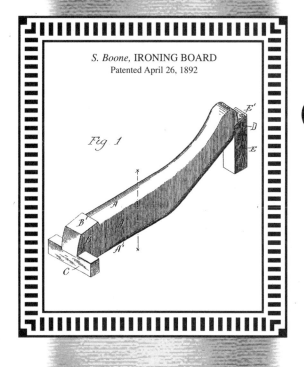

S. Boone, IRONING BOARD
Patented April 26, 1892

Fig 1

1 8 0 0 s

Sarah Boone invented the ironing board. Her board consisted of a smooth, heat-proof, narrow board with two curved edges. The ironing board was invented to provide an effective, simple, cheap, and convenient device for the purpose of ironing the sleeves and bodies of ladies' garments. Sarah Boone's invention was patented in 1892 and is still used throughout the world today. Prior to her invention, wooden boards or tables were set across chairs to iron clothes.

Sarah Boone lived in New Haven, Connecticut, at the time of her patent. It is hard to find more information on Sarah—even her birth date!

Lesson 4-2
Sarah Boone
Ironing Board

Skill Areas:
Language, Cognitive, Gross Motor, Fine Motor, Social, Visual Motor

Circle Time:
Have on display an ironing board and iron—possibly already part of your Housekeeping Center. If possible, bring in a real iron for children to examine as well. Discuss vocabulary words (*hot/cold*, *wet/dry*, *left/right*, and *up/down*). Explain to the children that Sarah Boone, an African American woman, invented the ironing board.

Fine Motor:
■ Provide catalogs and advertisements from department and grocery stores. Encourage children to locate and cut out pictures of irons, spray starch, clothes, and ironing boards.

Creative:
■ Children can color the modern picture of an ironing board on p. 79. Ask children to draw someone they know ironing.

Dramatic Play:
■ Have available in the Housekeeping Center a clothes basket with clothes for children to use to role play ironing.

■ Teach children how to iron using a toy iron and board and a garment. Let each child have a turn.

Snack:

Hot Cocoa

There are many cocoa trees in the rain forests of Africa. Farmers chop large pods from cocoa trees, cut open the pods, and take out the cocoa beans. The beans are fermented, dried either in the sun or by artificial heat, and then bagged for shipment and sold. The chocolate we eat comes from those beans. In the country of Ghana, cocoa is the most important crop, accounting for more than 60 percent of the total money earned by export.

Recipe:

> ### Hot Cocoa
> **(Serves 8–10)**
>
> *1/2 c water*
>
> *1 qt milk*
>
> *1/4 c cocoa*
>
> *1/2 c sugar*

Heat water and milk to almost boiling. Add cocoa and sugar and stir. Test temperature before serving.

Sarah Boone invented the ironing board. Her board consisted of a smooth, heat–proof, narrow board with two curved edges. The ironing board was invented to provide an effective, simple, cheap, and convenient device for the purpose of ironing the sleeves and bodies of ladies' garments. Sarah Boone's invention was patented in 1892 and is still used throughout the world today.

George T. Sampson

G.T. Sampson, CLOTHES DRIER
Patented June 7, 1892

1 8 0 0 s

George T. Sampson invented the clothes dryer. His dryer had a combination of frames for drying and supporting clothes. It included a long pan that was used as a receptacle for wet clothes. The purpose of Sampson's invention was to suspend clothing in close relation to a stove by means of frames. The clothes dryer was constructed so that it could be readily placed in proper position and put aside when not being used. Sampson received a patent for his invention on June 7, 1892. He lived in Dayton, Ohio, at the time of his invention. It is difficult to find personal information on George.

Lesson 4-3
George T. Sampson
Clothes Dryer

Skill Areas:
Language, Cognitive, Visual Motor, Gross Motor, Fine Motor, Social

Circle:
Invite the children to talk about their experiences doing laundry at home or at self-service laundries. Discuss all the steps involved in doing laundry, such as sorting, washing, drying, ironing, and folding. Explain to the children that the clothes dryer was invented by George T. Sampson, an African American man.

Creative:
Provide two large boxes to make a washing machine and clothes dryer. Cut a hole in the side of each box, leaving one section attached to create a flap that can open and close like a door. Draw a few dials and switches, and invite children to paint the machine.

Fine Motor:
Have children color the modern clothes dryer on p. 83. Ask them to draw other things that belong in a laundry room on the shelf above the dryer.

Dramatic Play:
Encourage children to create a self-service laundry. Provide baskets, clothes, magazines, an ironing board, detergent boxes, table, and an egg timer (used to tell when the laundry is "done"). Encourage cooperation by suggesting that children sort and wash their laundry together.

Gross Motor:
Have children bounce, catch, and throw a large ball into a laundry basket.

Story:
A Pocket for Corduroy

Snack:

Homemade Peanut Butter on Crackers

Have children wash hands and help prepare snack.

Recipe:

> ## Homemade Peanut Butter
> ### (Makes 1 cup)
>
> 1 1/2 c salted roasted peanuts
> 1 T oil
> 1 tsp honey

Put all ingredients into a blender and blend to the desired consistency. Let children spread peanut butter on crackers, and serve.

George T. Sampson

Name _____

George T. Sampson invented the clothes dryer. The purpose of Sampson's invention was to suspend clothing in close relation to a stove by means of frames. The clothes dryer was constructed so that it could be readily placed in proper position and put aside when not being used.

Jan E. Matzeliger

Jan E. Matzeliger
Shoe Lasting Machine   No.274,207
Patented March 20,1883

29
Black Heritage USA

1852 – 1889

Jan E. Matzeliger invented the shoe-lasting machine. This machine could sew the upper part of a shoe to the sole, thereby producing thousands of pairs of shoes in one day. By hand, skilled workers were able to make only forty to fifty pairs of shoes per day. Matzeliger's invention caused the shoe industry to increase production from one million to eleven million pairs a year. Before developing his invention, Matzeliger worked as an apprentice to a shoemaker in Philadelphia. Later he settled in Lynn, Massachusetts, where he worked in a shoe factory. In 1883 Matzeliger received a patent for his shoe-lasting machine. Shown above left is a photograph of a U.S. postage stamp with his picture, which was designed to honor him and his invention.

Lesson 4-4
Jan E. Matzeliger
Shoe-Lasting Machine

Skill Areas:

Language, Cognitive, Visual, Gross Motor, Fine Motor, Social

Circle:

Seat children in a circle with legs extended forward. Ask children to look at their shoes and observe how they are made. Discuss and look at the tops, sides, bottoms, and so on. Give children an opportunity to comment. Discuss the different types of shoes children are wearing and encourage them to identify similarities and differences. Have children count how many are wearing shoes with laces and how many are wearing shoes without. Discuss how early shoes were sewn by hand. Introduce Jan Matzeliger as a famous African American man and describe his invention.

Creative:

Using the shoe pattern on p. 87, precut the sole from both foam and cardboard. Cut the straps (p. 88) from felt. Next, have children glue the soles together and then glue the straps to the sole to create a sandal shoe.

Fine Motor:

Have children color the picture of Jan Matzeliger on p. 89. Encourage them to share the picture and their new information about Mr. Matzeliger with their parents.

Dramatic Play:

Provide children with different types of shoes (e.g., tennis shoes, boots, high heels, house slippers, rubbers, and pumps) to try on and tell who would wear them. Encourage children to create a shoe store and role-play the parts of customers, salespeople, cashiers, and so on.

Gross Motor:

Children can run a relay race, learning how tennis shoes allow more flexibility.

Story:

Red Dancing Shoes

Song:

Shoes

Tune: "I Got Shoes" (Spiritual)

(If children are not familiar with tune, have them recite verse as a poem.)

Red shoes, black shoes!
All the little children have shoes.
Let's get together and put on our shoes,
And walk a-round, walk a-round.
Let's get together and put on our shoes,
And walk all a-round.

—Dr. Mark H. Davis

Snack:

Sweet Potato Chips

Sweet potatoes are grown in tropical areas of Africa, the United States, and elsewhere. The part we eat is actually the root. Sweet potatoes are also called *yams*.

Sweet Potato Chips

2–4 sweet potatoes
non-stick cooking spray
salt

Preheat oven to 350° F. Scrub the potatoes with a brush and then peel. Cut them into 1/4" slices. Spray cookie sheet and then lay potatoes in a single layer along it. Spray tops of potatoes lightly with spray and salt lightly. Bake for 20 minutes. Turn slices over. Respray and bake another 20 minutes. Serve.

Field Trip:

Arrange a visit to a store where a variety of shoes are sold.

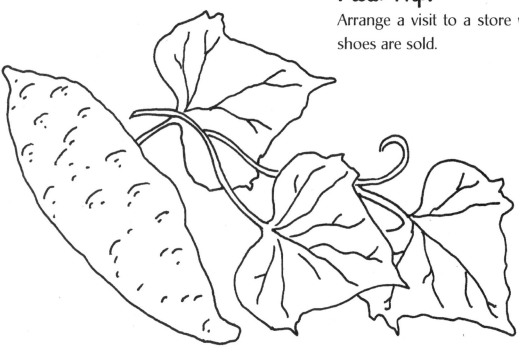

Jan E. Matzeliger

Pattern: Shoe Soles

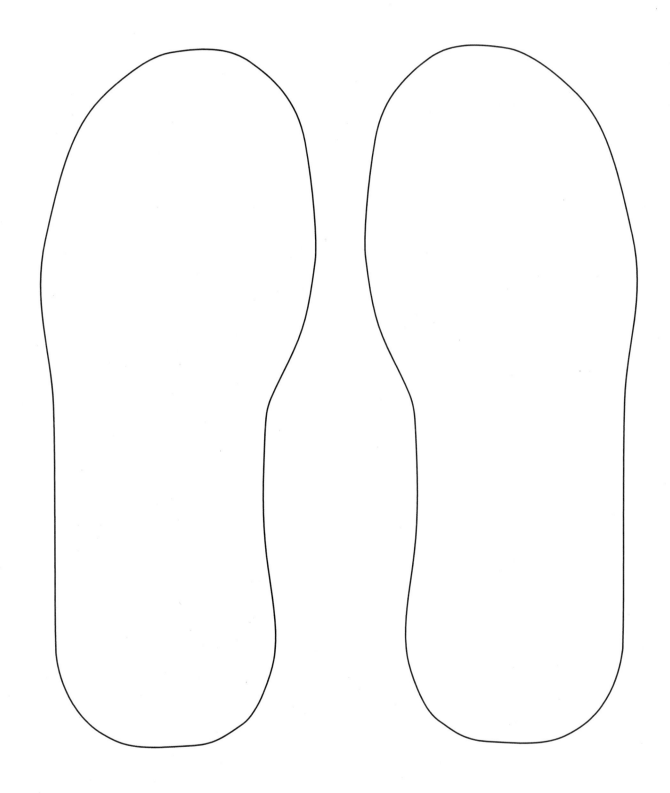

Jan E. Matzeliger

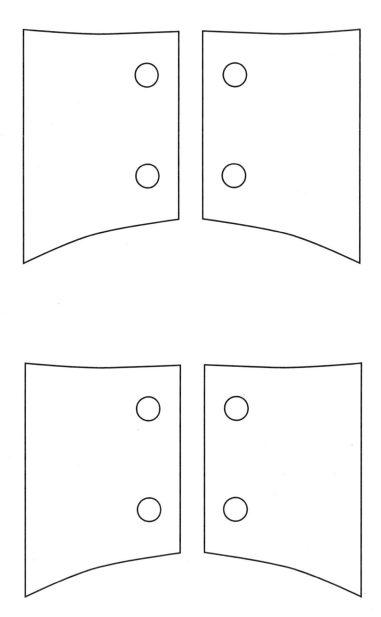

Jan E. Matzeliger

Jan E. Matzeliger invented the shoe-lasting machine. This machine could sew the upper part of a shoe to the sole, thereby producing thousands of pairs of shoes in one day. By hand, skilled workers were able to make only forty to fifty pairs of shoes per day. Matzeliger's invention caused the shoe industry to increase production from one million to eleven million pairs a year.

John W. Hunter

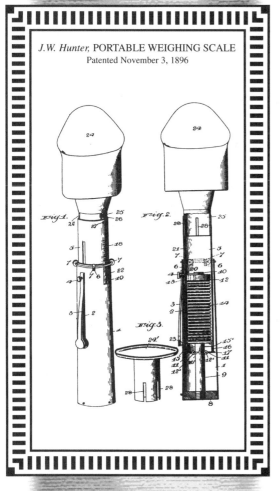

J.W. Hunter, PORTABLE WEIGHING SCALE
Patented November 3, 1896

1800s

John W. Hunter invented the portable weighing scale. He received a patent on November 3, 1896. Hunter's invention improved weighing scales for retail dealers and provided a simple, cheap, and reliable hand-portable scale. The weighing scale was used for weighing items such as flour, sugar, butter, and lard. The portable weighing scale sold for about $1.50, while counter scales retailed from $3.50 to $25.00. John Hunter lived in Tabor, Iowa, at the time of his patent and was a shoemaker.

Lesson 4-5
John W. Hunter
Scale

Skill Areas:

Language, Cognitive, Visual, Gross Motor, Fine Motor, Social

Circle:

Introduce this lesson by bringing in a weighing scale. Show the scale and ask, "What is this? What do we do with a scale?" Discuss the different types of scales and what they are used for. Ask children where they may have seen scales in use (e.g., a doctor's office, grocery store, pharmacy, or truck weighing station). Explain to children that John W. Hunter, an African American, invented the portable weighing scale.

Fine Motor:

- Have children make a coat-hanger scale. Hang a small, empty plastic basket on each end of a coat hanger. Children can place small objects in the baskets and discuss concepts such as *more* and *less*. Use objects such as crayons and small blocks for weighing.

- Have children color the pictures of scales on page 93. Ask them their own weight, and have them fill in the bathroom scale to match their weight. If possible, provide a scale to weigh children who would like to check their weight.

Dramatic Play:

Encourage children to wash their hands and then pretend to be chefs. Provide children with a scale and measuring utensils and let them assist in preparing their snack by trying to measure ingredients.

Snack:

Fruit Cocktail

Bring a scale to class for measuring portions. Find out how much fruit cocktail fills a small paper cup. Then measure this exact amount into subsequent cups so everyone has the same portion.

Story:

Straight Hair, Curly Hair

Field Trip:

Visit a doctor's office or clinic. Speak with the doctor or nurse and observe the scale and other instruments. As an alternative, arrange a visit to the school nurse.

John W. Hunter

African American Awareness for Young Children, Copyright © 1999 Good Year Books.

Name _____

MY WEIGHT:

John W. Hunter invented the portable weighing scale. Hunter's invention improved weighing scales for retail dealers and provided a simple, cheap, and reliable hand-portable scale. The weighing scale was used for weighing items such as flour, sugar, butter, and lard.

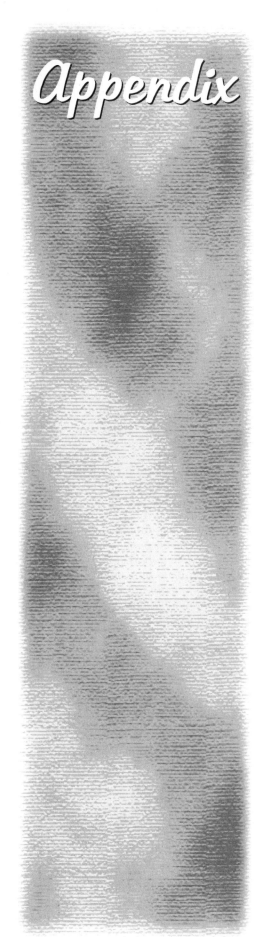

Appendix

Reference Materials

CONTENTS

Children's Books
■ African American Children's Books

Authors
■ Famous Authors of African American Children's Books

Illustrators
■ Famous African American Illustrators

Publishers
■ Famous African American Publishers

Catalogs and Suppliers
■ Catalogs and Suppliers Specializing in African American Educational Products

Museums
■ Museums of African American Arts

African American Awareness for Young Children, Copyright © 1999 Good Year Books.

Children's Books

African American Children's Books

Aardena, Verna. *Bimwili and the Zimwili.* Dial Books for Young Readers, 1985.

———. *Bringing the Rain to Kapiti Plain.* Dial Books for Young Readers, 1985.

———. *Oh, Kojo! How Could You?* Dial Books for Young Readers, 1984.

———. *Who's in Rabbit's House?* Dial Books for Young Readers, 1977.

———. *Why Mosquitoes Buzz in People's Ears.* Dial Books for Young Readers, 1975.

Adler, David A. *A Picture Book of Martin Luther King, Jr.* Holiday House, 1989.

Adoff, Arnold. *Black Is Brown Is Tan.* Harper, 1973.

———. *Mandala.* Harper and Row, 1971.

Aliki. *A Weed Is a Flower: The Life of George Washington Carver.* Simon and Schuster, 1988.

Asare, Meshack. *Cat in Search of a Friend.* Kane/Miller Book Publishers, 1986.

Bang, Molly. *Ten, Nine, Eight.* William Morrow, 1991.

———. *Yellow Ball.* William Morrow, 1991.

Banks, Valerie J. *Flags of the African People: Banderas of the African Diaspora.* Sala Enterprises, 1990.

Benjamin, Anne. *Young Harriet Tubman: Freedom Fighter.* Troll Associates, 1992.

———. *Young Rosa Parks.* Troll Associates, 1996.

Bogart, Jo-Ellen. *Daniel's Dog.* Scholastic, 1980.

Bowden, Joan. *Why Do the Sun and the Moon Live in the Sky?* Houghton Mifflin, 1968.

———. *Why the Tides Ebb and Flow.* Houghton Mifflin, 1989.

Bradman, Tony. *The Bad Babies' Counting Book.* Knopf, 1986.

Brains, Rae. *Martin Luther King, Jr.* Troll Associates, 1995.

Brown, Margaret W. *Baby Animals.* Random House, 1989.

Bryan, Ashley. *Beat the Story-Drum, Pum-Pum.* Macmillan, 1987.

———. *The Dancing Granny.* Macmillan, 1987.

Children's Books (continued)

———. *Turtle Knows Your Name.* Macmillan, 1989.

Caines, Jeannette. *Abby.* Harper Collins, 1984.

———. *Just Us Women.* Harper Collins, 1984.

Calloway, Northern. *I Been There.* Doubleday, 1982.

Cameron, Ann. *More Stories Julian Tells.* Knopf, 1986.

———. *The Stories Julian Tells.* Pantheon, 1981.

Carlstrom, Nancy W. *Wild Wild Sunflower Child Anna.* New York: Macmillan, 1987.

Cauper, Eunice. *Martin Luther King Jr. and Our January 15th Holiday for Children.* Eunice Cauper, 1991.

Clifton, Lucille. *All Us Come Cross the Water.* Holt, 1973.

———. *Everett Anderson's 1-2-3.* Holt, 1997.

———. *Everett Anderson's Christmas Coming.* Holt, 1991.

———. *Everett Anderson's Friend.* Holt, 1992.

———. *Everett Anderson's Goodbye.* Holt, 1988.

———. *Everett Anderson's Nine Month Long.* Holt, 1978.

———. *Some of the Days of Everett Anderson.* Holt, 1988.

———. *Everett Anderson's Year.* Holt, 1992.

Crews, Donald. *School Bus.* Morrow, 1993.

Crump, Fred. *Afrotina and the Three Bears*: A Retold Story. Winston-Derek, 1991.

———. *Cinderella: A Retold Story.* Winston-Derek, 1990.

———. *Hakim and Grenita: A Retold Story.* Winston-Derek, 1991.

———. *Jamako and the Beanstalk: A Retold Story.* Winston-Derek, 1992.

———. *Little Red Riding Hood: A Retold Story.* Winston-Derek, 1989.

———. *Mother Goose: A Retold Story.* Winston-Derek, 1990.

———. *Rose for Zamira.* Winston-Derek, 1989.

Daly, Niki. *Not So Fast, Sungololo.* Macmillan, 1986.

Dee, Ruby. *Two Ways to Count to Ten.* Holt , 1990.

De Veaus, Alexis. *An Enchanted Hair Tale.* Harper Collins, 1987.

Dobrin, Arnold. *Josephine's Imagination: A Tale of Haiti.* Scholastic, 1991.

Children's Books (continued)

Dragonwagon, Crescent. *Half a Moon and One Whole Star.* Macmillan, 1990.

———. *Home Place.* Macmillan, 1990.

Farrell, Edward. *Young Jackie Robinson.* Troll Associates, 1992.

Feelings, Muriel. *Jambo Means Hello: Swahili Alphabet Book.* Dial, 1985.

———. *Moja Means One: A Swahili Counting Book.* Dial, 1987.

———. *Something on My Mind.* Dial, 1978.

Fitzgerald, Elizabeth. *Aunt Flossie's Hats.* Clarion Books, 1991.

Florian, Douglas. *Discovering Trees.* Macmillan, 1990.

Flournoy, Valerie. *The Patchwork Quilt.* Dial, 1985.

Freeman, Don. *Corduroy.* Puffin, 1993.

———. *A Pocket for Corduroy.* Puffin, 1993.

Giles, Lucille. *Color Me Brown.* Johnson, 1974

Goldin, Augusta. *Straight Hair, Curly Hair.* Harper Collins, 1966.

Gomi, Taro. *Coco Can't Wait.* Puffin Books, 1985.

Greene, Carole. *Martin Luther King, Jr.: A Man Who Changed Things.* Childrens Press, 1989.

———. *Jackie Robinson: Baseball's First Black Major Leaguer.* Childrens Press, 1990.

Greenfield, Eloise. *Africa Dream.* Harper Collins, 1989.

———. *Daydreamers.* Dial, 1981.

———. *Grandmama's Joy.* Philomel, 1980.

———. *Grandpa's Face.* Philomel, 1991.

———. *Honey, I Love: And Other Love Poems.* Harper Collins Children's Books, 1986.

———. *Me and Nessie.* Harper Collins, 1984.

———. *Nathaniel Talking.* Writers and Readers, 1993.

———. *She Come Bringing Me That Little Baby Girl.* Harper Collins, 1993.

———. *Under the Sunday Tree.* Harper Trophy, 1991.

———. *Young Rosa Parks.* Troll, 1996.

Grifalconi, Ann. *Osa's Pride.* Little, Brown, 1990.

———. *Village of Round and Square Houses.* Little, Brown, 1986.

Hailey, Gail. *A Story, a Story.* Atheneum, 1970.

Hamilton, Virginia. *The People Could Fly.* Knopf, 1993.

Children's Books (continued)

Haskins, Jim. *Count Your Way Through Africa.* Carolrhoda, 1989.

Havill, Juanita. *Jamaica's Find.* Houghton Mifflin, 1986.

———. *Jamaica Tag-Along.* Houghton Mifflin, 1989.

Hayes, Sarah. *Eat Up, Gemma.* William Morrow, 1994.

Hoffman, Mary. *Amazing Grace.* Dial, 1991.

Hoffman, Phyllis. *We Play.* Harper Collins, 1990.

Hudson, Cheryl W. *Afro-Bets Book A B C.* Just Us Books, 1987.

Hudson, Cheryl W., and Bernette G. Ford. *Bright Eyes, Brown Skin.* Just Us Books, 1990.

Hudson, Wade, et al. *Jamal's Busy Day.* Just Us Books, 1991.

Isadora, Rachel. *Ben's Trumpet.* Greenwillow, 1979.

———. *Friends.* Greenwillow Books, 1990.

James, Cynthia S.. *The Gifts of Kwanzaa.* Albert Whitman & Company, 1994.

Johnson, Angela. *Do Like Kyla.* Orchard Books, 1990.

Jonas, Ann. *The Quilt.* Greenwillow, 1984.

———. *When I Am Old with You.* Orchard Books, 1982.

———. *When You Were a Baby.* Greenwillow, 1982.

Keats, Ezra Jack. *Apartment 3.* Macmillan, 1986.

———. *Goggles!* Macmillan, 1987.

———. *Hi, Cat!* Macmillan, 1988.

———. *John Henry: An American Legend.* Knopf, 1987.

———. *A Letter to Amy.* Harper Collins, 1984.

———. *Pet Show!* Macmillan, 1974.

———. *Peter's Chair.* Harper, 1967.

———. *The Snowy Day.* Puffin, 1976.

———. *Whistle for Willie.* Puffin Books, 1976.

Kelly, Keith. *Basketball Jones.* Atheneum, 1980.

Knutson, Barbara. *Why the Crab Has No Head: An African Folktale.* Carolrhoda Books, 1987.

Kurtz, Jane. *I'm Calling Molly.* Albert Whitman and Company, 1990.

Lewin, Hugh. *Jafta.* Lerner, 1989.

———. *Jafta's Father.* Lerner, 1989.

———. *Jafta's Mother.* Lerner, 1989.

Children's Books (continued)

———. *Jafta: The Journey*. Carolrhoda, 1984.

———. *Jafta: The Town*. Carolrhoda Books, 1984.

Lexau, Joan. *Don't Be My Valentine*. Harper Collins, 1985.

Lillegard, Dee. *My First Martin Luther King Book*. Childrens Press, 1987.

Little, Lessie. *Children of Long Ago*. Philomel Books, 1988.

Little, Lessie, and Eloise Greenfield. *I Can Do It by Myself*. Harper Collins, 1978.

Martin, Bill. *I Am Freedom's Child*. Bowmar, 1970.

Marzollo, Jean. *Pretend You're a Cat*. Dial, 1990.

Mathis, Sharon. *The Hundred-Penny Box*. Viking Press, 1975.

Mattern, Joanne. *Young Martin Luther King, Jr.: I Have a Dream*. Troll Associates, 1992.

McDermott, Gerald. *Anansi the Spider: A Tale from the Ashanti*, retold and illustrated. Holt, 1987.

McKissack, Patricia C. *Flossie and the Fox*. Dial, 1986.

———. *A Million Fish…More or Less*. Knopf, 1992.

———. *Mirandy and Brother Wind*. Knopf, 1988.

———. *Nettie Jo's Friends*. Knopf, 1989.

———. *Who Is Who?* Childrens Press, 1983.

McKissack, Patricia, and Frederick McKissack. *The Big Bug Book of Opposites*. Milliken, 1987.

———. *Country Mouse and City Mouse*. Childrens Press, 1985

———. *Messy Bessey*. Childrens Press, 1987.

———. *The Three Bears*. Childrens Press, 1985.

Mendez, Phil. *The Black Snowman*. Scholastic, 1989.

Mitchell, Barbara. *A Pocketful of Goobers: A Story About George Washington Carver*. Carolrhoda, 1986.

Monjo, F. N. *The Drinking Gourd*. Harper Collins, 1983.

Morninghouse, Sundaira. *Nightfeathers: Black Goose Rhymes*. Open Hand, 1989.

Musgrove, Margaret W. *Ashanti to Zulu: African Traditions*. Dial, 1976.

Myers, Walter D. *Mr. Monkey and the Gotcha Bird*. Delacorte Press, 1982.

———. *Young Martin's Promise*. Raintree, 1992.

Newton, Deborah. *My First Kwanzaa Books*. Scholastic, 1992.

Children's Books (continued)

Omerad, Jan. *Young Joe.* Lothrop, Lee and Shepard, 1986.

Patrick, Denise. *Red Dancing Shoes.* Mulberry, 1993.

Peck, Ira. *The Life and Words of Martin Luther King, Jr.* Scholastic, 1991.

Petrie, Catherine. *Joshua James Likes Trucks.* Childrens Press, 1982.

Pomerantz, Charlotte. *The Chalk Doll.* Harper Collins, 1993.

Pragoff, Fiona. *Opposites.* Doubleday, 1989.

Price, Leontyne. *Aida.* Harcourt Brace Jovanovich, 1990.

Ringgold, Faith. *Tar Beach.* Crown, 1994.

Samuels, Vyanne. *Carry Go Bring Come.* Macmillan, 1989.

Scott, Ann. H. *Sam.* Putnam, 1992.

Seed, Jenny. *Ntombi's Song.* Beacon Press, 1987.

Seeger, Pete. *Abiyoyo.* Macmillan, 1994.

Sendak, Maurice. *Where the Wild Things Are.* Harper Collins, 1992.

Shelby, Anne. *We Keep a Store.* Orchard Books, 1990.

Showers, Paul. *Your Skin and Mine.* Harper Collins, 1991.

Simon, Norma. *Oh, That Cat!* Albert Whitman, 1986.

Slier, Debbie. *Animal Noises.* Checkerboard Press, 1990.

———. *Baby's Games.* Checkerboard Press, 1990.

———. *Hello School.* Checkerboard Press, 1990.

———. *Little Babies.* Checkerboard Press, 1989.

———. *Me and My Dad.* Checkerboard Press, 1990.

———. *My Noisy Book.* Checkerboard Press, 1990.

Smith, Jean P. *Li'l Tuffy and His ABC's.* Johnson, 1973.

Smith, Kathie B. *Harriet Tubman.* Simon & Shuster, 1989.

Steptoe, John. *Baby Says.* Lothrop, Lee and Shepard, 1988.

———. *Daddy Is a Monster Sometimes.* Harper Collins, 1980.

———. *Mufaro's Beautiful Daughters.* Lothrop, Lee and Shepard, 1987.

———. *Stevie.* Harper Collins, 1969.

———. *The Story of Jumping Mouse.* Lothrop, Lee and Shepard, 1984.

Thompson, Marguerite. *Martin Luther King, Jr.: A Story for Children.* Dare, 1983.

Children's Books (continued)

Tierney, Tom. *Famous African-American Women Paper Dolls.* Dover, 1994.

Udry, Janice M. *What Mary Jo Shared.* Scholastic, 1991.

Ward, Leila. *I Am Eyes Ni Macho.* Scholastic, 1987.

Williams, Vera B. *Cherries and Cherry Pits.* Greenwillow, 1986.

———. *More, More, More, Said the Baby.* Greenwillow, 1990.

Wilson, Beth. *Jenny.* Macmillan's Children's Books, 1990.

African American Awareness for Young Children, Copyright © 1999 Good Year Books.

Authors

■ ■ ■ ■ ■ ■ ■ ■ ■ ■ ■ ■ ■ ■ ■ ■ ■ ■ ■ ■

Famous Authors of African American Children's Books

(not all inclusive)

Aardena, Verna
Adler, David A.
Adoff, Arnold
Aliki
Asare, Meshack
Bang, Molly
Banks, Valerie J.
Benjamin, Anne
Bogart, Jo-Ellen
Bowden, Joan
Bradman, Tony
Brains, Rae
Brown, Margaret
Bryan, Ashley
Caines, Jeannette
Calloway, Northern
Cameron, Ann
Carlstrom, Nancy
Clifton, Lucille
Crews, Donald
Crump, Fred
Daly, Niki
Dee, Ruby
De Veaus, Alexis
Dobrin, Arnold
Dragonwagon, Crescent
Farrell, Edward
Feelings, Muriel
Fitzgerald, Elizabeth
Florian, Douglas
Flournoy, Valerie
Ford, Bernette
Freeman, Don

Giles, Lucille
Goldin, Augusta
Gomi, Taro
Greene, Carol
Greenfield, Eloise
Grifalconi, Ann
Hailey, Gail
Hamilton, Virginia
Haskins, Jim
Havill, Juanita
Hayes, Sarah
Hoffman, Mary
Hoffman, Phyllis
Hudson, Cheryl W.
Hudson, Wade
Isadora, Rachel
James, Cynthia S.
Johnson, Angela
Jonas, Ann
Keats, Ezra Jack
Kelly, Keith
Knutson, Barbara
Kurtz, Jane
Lewin, Hugh
Lexau, Joan
Lillegard, Dee
Little, Lessie
Martin, Bill
Marzollo, Jean
Mathis, Sharon
Mattern, Joanne
McDermott, Gerald
McKissack, Patricia C.

Mendez, Phil
Mitchell, Barbara
Monjo, F. N.
Morninghouse, Sundaira
Musgrove, Margaret W.
Myers, Walter D.
Newton, Deborah
Omerad, Jan
Peck, Ira
Petrie, Catherine
Pomerantz, Charlotte
Pragoff, Fiona
Price, Leontyne
Ringgold, Faith
Samuels, Vyanne
Scott, Ann H.
Seeds, Jenny
Seeger, Pete
Sendak, Maurice
Shelby, Anne
Showers, Paul
Simon, Norma
Slier, Debbie
Smith, Jean P.
Smith, Kathie B.
Steptoe, John
Thompson, Marguerite
Tierney, Tom
Tonra, Illan
Udry, Janice
Ward, Leila
Williams, Vera B.

■ ■ ■ ■ ■ ■ ■ ■ ■ ■ ■ ■ ■ ■ ■ ■ ■ ■ ■ ■

Illustrators

Famous African American Illustrators

(not all inclusive)

Asare, Meshack	Fields, Theodore
Bang, Molly	Ford, George
Barbett, Monete	Fufuka, Mahri
Bearden, Romare	Gilchrist, Jan Spivey
Bible, Charles	Hudson, Cheryl W.
Bryan, Ashley	Jefferson, Sharon
Byard, Carole	Jenkins, Maurice
Cummings, Pat	Parks, Gordon M.
Depillards, Murry N.	Pinkney, J.
Dillon, Diane	Steptoe, John
Dillon, Leo	Wesley, Valerie Wilson
Douglas, Aaron	Wilson, John
Feelings, Tom	

Publishers

....

African American Publishers

Publishers of Specifically African American Children's Books

Black Butterfly Press
PO Box 461 Village Station
New York, NY 10014
(212) 982-3158

Charill Publications
44-68 San Francisco Ave.
St. Louis, MO 63115
(314) 382-4998

Empak Publications
212 E. Ohio St.
Chicago, IL 60611
(312) 642-3434

Johnson Publishing Company
1820 S. Michigan Avenue
Chicago, IL 60605
(312) 322-9200

Just Us Books
356 Glenwood Ave.
3rd Floor
East Orange, NJ 07017
(973) 676-9200

Maral Enterprises
PO Box 361
New York, NY 10028
(212) 348-7080

Third World Press
7822 S. Dobson
Chicago, IL 60619-1999
(773) 651-0700

Catalogs and Suppliers

Catalogs and Suppliers
Specializing in African American Educational Products

Afro-American Distributing Company
819 S. Wabash Ave.
Chicago, IL 60605
(puzzles, games, posters, and books for adults and children with an Afrocentric emphasis)

Afro-Centric Expressions
8081 Olive Blvd.
St. Louis, MO 63130
(314) 991-0097
(books, gifts, Afrocentric items and arts, specializing in black books)

Alkebu-Lan Images
2721 Jefferson St.
Nashville, TN 37208
(615) 321-4111
(educational materials depicting African Americans)

Constructive Playthings
1227 East 119th St.
Grandview, MO 64030-1117
1-800-448-4115
Fax: (816) 761-9295
(culturally diverse materials for anti-bias curriculum)

Identity Toys, Inc.
2821 N. 4th Street
Milwaukee, WI 53212
(books, dolls, games, puzzles that develop pride and self-esteem)

Lakeshore Learning Materials
2695 E. Dominguez St.
Carson, CA 90749
1-800-421-5354
(multicultural educational materials for early childhood)

Multi-Cultural Program Materials
New England School Supply
PO Box 1581
Springfield, MA 01101-1581
(books and crafts on African Americans)

Multi-Media Education
19363 Livernois
Detroit, MI 48221
1-800-342-1261
(materials for building racial pride and promoting interracial understanding)

National Women's History Project
7738 Bell Road
Windsong, CA 95492-8518
(707) 838-6000
(educational materials honoring women's history)

Progressive Emporium
6265 Delmar Blvd.
St. Louis, MO 63130
(314) 721-1344
(Afrocentric books, games, and arts)

Museums

Museums of African American Arts

Afro-American Cultural and Historical Museum
7th & Arch Streets
Philadelphia, PA 19108
(215) 574-0380

The Black Inventions Museum
Sala Enterprises
PO Box 76122
Los Angeles, CA 90076
(310) 859-4602

Black World History Wax Museum
2505 St. Louis Ave.
St. Louis, MO 63106
(314) 241-7057

National Museum of African Art
Smithsonian Institute
950 Independence Ave. S.W.
Washington, D.C.
(202) 357-1300

The Museum of Black Inventors
7th South Newstead
St. Louis, MO 63108
(314) 533-1333

The Studio Museum of Harlem
144 W. 125th St
New York, NY 10027
(212) 864-4500

African American Awareness for Young Children, Copyright © 1999 Good Year Books.

Bibliography

Benson, Janice E. Hale. *Black Children: Their Roots, Culture and Learning Styles.* Johns Hopkins University, 1986.

———. "Vision for Children: African American Early Childhood Education Program." *Early Childhood Research Quarterly,* 5, 199-213, 1990.

Bredekamp, Sue. *Developmentally Appropriate Practice in Early Childhood Programs Serving Children from Birth Through Age 8.* NAEYC, 1834 Connecticut Avenue, N.W., Washington, DC 20009, 1986.

Burt, Minkley. *Black Inventors of America.* National Book Company, 1989.

Dunfee, M. "Ethnic Modification of the Curriculum." *Association for Supervision and Curriculum Development.* Washington, DC: National Educational Association (NEA), 1970.

Garrett, Romes B. *Famous First Facts About Negroes. New York:* Anno Press, 1972.

Goodman, Mary E. *Race Awareness in Young Children.* Collier Books, 1964.

Green, Richard L. *A Salute to Black Scientists and Inventors.* Empak, 1985.

Harber, Louis. *Black Pioneers of Science and Invention.* Harcourt Brace & World, Inc., 1970.

Hraba, J., and G. Grant. "Black Is Beautiful: A Re-examination of Racial Preferences and Identification." *Journal of Personality and Social Psychology,* vol. 16, 1970.

Kimmel, E. A. *Can Children's Books Change Children's Values?* Island Press, 1970.

Klein, Aaron E. *The Hidden Contributors: Black Scientists and Inventors in America.* Doubleday, 1971.

Litchner, John H., and Davis W. Johnson. "Change in Attitudes Toward Negroes of White Elementary School Students After Use Of Multi-Ethnic Readers." *Journal of Educational Psychology,* LX, 1969.

Mabry, Marcus, and Patrick Rogers. "Bias Begins At Home: A Disturbing Study About Black Images." *Newsweek,* 33, August 1991.

Purkey, W. W. *Self-Concept and School Achievement.* Prentice Hall, Inc., 1970.

Rudman, Marsha Kabakou. *Children's Literature: An Issue Approach.* D. C. Heath, 1976.

Westcott, Nadine Bernard. *Peanut Butter and Jelly (A Play Rhyme).* E. P. Dutton, 1992.

Williams, James C. *At Last Recognition: A Reference Handbook of Unknown Black Inventors and Their Contributions to America.* B.C.A. Publishing Company, 1978.

Wilson, R. "Intellectually and Philosophically, We Must Divorce Educational Achievement from Cultural Afffirmation." *The Chronicle of Higher Education,* 37 (47), B1–B3, August 1991.

Winslow, Eugene. *Black Americans in Science and Engineering.* Afro-AM Publishing Company, Inc., 1984.

About the Author

Dr. Evia L. Davis is presently a preschool coordinator for the St. Louis Public School System. She has been with the district for over 15 years and has taught kindergarten, fourth, and fifth grades. She is also an adjunct professor at Harris-Stowe State College. Davis holds life certification in six areas: Learning Disabled K–12, Early Childhood Education preK–3, Early Childhood Special Education K–3, Mentally Handicapped K–12, Behavioral Disorder K–12, as well as Elementary Education 1–8.

Davis has a bachelor's degree in Elementary Education from Langston University, in Langston, Oklahoma. She received her master's degree in Child Development from Washington State University in Pullman, Washington, and her doctorate in Early Childhood Education from St. Louis University in St. Louis, Missouri.

The author is a member of New Sunny Mount Baptist Church, the National Black Child Development Association, National Association for Education of Young Children, and Association for Childhood Education International, and Delta Sigma Theta Sorority.

Evia is married to Dr. Mark Hosea Davis and they have two children, Nicole Titilayo Davis and Mark Hosea Davis II. The Davises are the founders of Akwaaba, Incorporated, a nonprofit organization that provides charitable support for the village of Gomoa Obuasi, Ghana (West Africa), as well as other worthy causes.